Series / Number 03-035

Public Labor Relations:
A Comparative State Study

D. S. CHAUHAN
University of Arkansas

with Mark Rounsavall

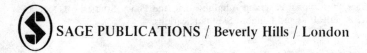

SAGE PUBLICATIONS / Beverly Hills / London

For information address:

SAGE PUBLICATIONS, INC.
275 South Beverly Drive
Beverly Hills, California 90212

SAGE PUBLICATIONS LTD
St George's House / 44 Hatton Garden
London EC1N 8ER

International Standard Book Number 0-8039-0629-3

Library of Congress Catalog Card No. 76-21915

FIRST PRINTING

When citing a professional paper, please use the proper form. Remember to cite the
correct Sage Professional Paper series title and include the paper number. One of the
two following formats can be adapted (depending on the style manual used):

(1) OSTROM, E. et al. (1973) "Community Organization and the Provision of Police
Services." Sage Professional Papers in Administrative and Policy Studies, 1, 03-001.
Beverly Hills and London: Sage Pubns.

OR

(2) Ostrom, Elinor, et al. 1973. *Community Organization and the Provision of Police
Services.* Sage Professional Papers in Administrative and Policy Studies, vol. 1, series
no. 03-001. Beverly Hills and London: Sage Publications.

CONTENTS

Public Labor Relations:
A Comparative State Study

D. S. CHAUHAN
University of Arkansas
with Mark Rounsavall

I. INTRODUCTION

Government employees have been growing increasingly militant for more than a decade. In 1960, there were 17 strikes involving 1,700 federal, state, and local workers. The rapid expansion of unionized activities reached the level of 375 strikes affecting 142,100 workers in 1972. The 700,000 member American Federation of State, County, and Municipal Employees (AFSCME) is the fastest growing labor union, gaining 1,000 new members a week (*Time*, July 1974: 41). Its leaders are lobbying hard in Congress for passage of a law that would guarantee public workers (except policemen and firemen) the right to strike. Meanwhile, a considerable number of state and local governments are not adequately prepared to cope up with the problem if the right to strike by public workers becomes a reality. Ironically, the current status of state policy regulations for managing public sector labor-management relations is characterized by inadequate legislative measures, lack of administrative procedures and mechanisms, negative attitudes towards the formation of public employee unions among lawmakers, public administrators, and the supporters of state sovereign rights.

THE PROCESS OF PUBLIC LABOR-MANAGEMENT RELATIONS

The process of labor-management relations in public sector employment involves a complex set of problems. Institutionally, the process involves two

AUTHOR'S NOTE: *Mark Rousavall worked on this project as a research assistant and helped to prepare the draft of this study. He is currently serving as a legislative analyst for the Arkansas Legislative Council. The typing assistance provided by Mrs. Elaine Craig and Mrs. Vicki Rounsavall is greatly appreciated.*

major actors: employer and employee groups and organizations. Numerous administrative agencies, employee groups, and organizations comprise these two sides and exert interacting influence while playing the game of collective bargaining in order to maximize gains in their own interests. Public employee unionization and bargaining have caused great concern for public officials because

(1) they involve questions of municipal, state, and federal legality; and

(2) they may entail the strike-long negotiation cycle that characterizes the private sector.

It is not unfair to assume that if public employee bargaining activities are unavoidable and will increase in the future, it is paramount that public personnel policies and public administrators in general should take a hard analytic look at labor-management relations process and seek improvement by establishing policies and regulatory norms to circumvent the difficulties that may emerge from the paralysis of public services and the hard bargaining process (Williams, 1972: 34).

Although private industry is well acquainted with employee unions and their activities, the development of employee unions or associations is relatively new in the public sector. Many states and municipalities are heading in this direction by establishing laws and procedures that recognize public employee unions or associations. Still, a considerable number of states and local governments do not have such laws or formal policies and procedures. Those state or local jurisdictions which do not have any legislative or regulatory measures are bound to face a formidable challenge from public employee unions or associations in the near future. Despite fears and suspicions towards unions among public managers, the need is growing for establishing necessary laws and procedures. A realistic appraisal of this growing phenomenon would indicate that public employee unions are becoming active partners in the modern public personnel management process. It is time now that politicians as well as public administrators stop debating about the pros and cons of public employee unions and start thinking positively along the lines of developing policies and regulatory norms.

THE DOGMA OF STATE SOVEREIGNTY

In the traditional pattern of thought on state sovereignty, it was emphasized that the sovereign character of government requires an absolute authoritative decision-making power. However, in a democracy such power should be legitimized by the support of the majority. Obviously, this view treats public unions as a countervailing force that would seriously undermine the basic premise of representative democracy and would interfere with the legitimate right of the government to conduct public business. An impartial observer of public affairs would fail to comprehend the significance of this view in the light of modern social change and strategic moves undertaken by the government to manage different crisis situations in public management (Gawthorp, 1971: 3-9; Nigro, 1973: 262-273). It is, however, important to note that in modern complex government it is the proper delegation of authority and cooperative endeavors that make the government work more effectively. For instance, in crisis situations, Congress has often delegated its constitutional powers to the executive or administrative branch without being dogmatic about the sovereign authority of the state.

The entire governmental business is a collaborative undertaking where both the major institutional components and individual administrative agencies play dynamic roles in promoting socioeconomic development. It is this dynamic of change that makes it very clear that the modern state cannot live up to people's expectations if it does not share its powers with other legitimate public institutions (Anderson, 1968: 24). Attacking on the dogmatic view of stage sovereignty Moskow et al. (1970) argue that the sovereignty of the state has already been compromised by many other factors such as government contracts, economic crises, legal opinions, and judicial decisions. Furthermore, government has long recognized the need to enter into contracts for the services of such professionals as doctors, engineers, and accountants. To argue that the government cannot contract for employment collectively would be very hard to defend (Moskow et al., 1970: 18).

It is also important to note that—in the context of modern socioeconomic changes—the interpretation of courts reflected in various judicial decisions does not support the old Hobbesian view of state sovereignty. Modern judicial policy recognizes the fact that the functional responsibilities of the government and the demands of citizens are quite diversified and complex. The state as a sovereign authority may not exclusively resort to iron-handed policy while dealing with its own employees. A strong adherence to the idea of "sovereign rights" may have counterproductive effects and promote disharmony between the government and its employees. What is paramount in this case is the "public interest" which could be best served by maintaining stable and harmonious relations between the two. Thus, enacting necessary laws and formulating required regulatory means become prime necessities in maintaining healthy relationships (Hampton, 1974: 5-9).

The impact of judicial policy on the changing phenomenon of state sovereignty and public-labor-management relations reflects a dynamic shift in the attitudes of judicial decision-makers.[1] A detailed discussion of this changing phenomenon is found in a recent thought-provoking research study conducted by Krajcik (1974: 83-94).

IMPACT OF SOME POPULAR ATTITUDES

There are a host of value concerns which characterize negative popular attitudes towards the formation of public employee unions. These concerns center around popular themes that the growth of unions will: undermine public interest, weaken the management decision-making power, promote professionalism, destroy merit system, enhance the power potential of unions, increase the threat to strike, and promote nonresponsive character in public management by giving primary importance to group interest.

One might ignore these concerns according to one's own value preference, but they are quite often repeated by analysts in the academic community as well as public observers. An analytical summary of various arguments will porvide a proper perspective concerning the impact of popular attitudes on legislative behavior in state and localities:

(1) People in general share the view that they are not adequately represented in negotiations between public labor and management (public administrators). Furthermore, public administrators form a class among themselves and bargaining as such takes place in secrecy. Along with this suspicion, the public often feels that they will pay the cost of any negotiated agreement without any representation (Zeidler, 1972: 3).

(2) The growth of public employee unions is viewed as direct conflict with the principles of merit system. Much has been written on this subject; while such fears may be soundly based, the destruction of merit system need not be inevitable. Some say that destruction can be neutralized by suitable modifications in merit principles and civil service laws (Zeidler, 1972: 2-3). Others maintain that there is no competition or conflict between union activity and the merity system (Spero and Capozzola, 1973: 211-212).

(3) Another concern involving public interest stems from the growth of professional associations among professional, technical, and administrative personnel. It is contended that this growth of professionalism will lead to increasing demands to influence policy matters in a particular state or locale (Zeidler, 1972: 4).

(4) Both public officials and the public suffer from a kind of fear or psychoneurosis of unions becoming too powerful. In its obvious extreme it means "unions contolling government." Government officials also feel that they will lose power and that increasing union activity will seriously undermine their decision-making authority. To the general public, the word "union" seems to be synonymous with strike. A city dweller does not want his garbage piled high on the street because the sanitation workers want higher wages. The union is often seen as an obstructionist organization.

While some of these arguments or fears may be well-founded, it must be noted that the basic opposition to the formation of public employee unions and subsequent union activity broadly stems from two prevailing attitudes:

(1) the government employer and the public in general almost automatically relate unions with strikes; and

(2) if not kept in close check or under restraint, public employee unions may acquire so much power as to become the final decision-makers, not only in collective negotiations concerning working conditions, but also in substantive policy areas.

These attitudes have tremendous impact on the policy of establishing necessary laws or regulatory measures in a particular state or locale. For instance, Arkansas and some other states which do not have any public labor management laws usually typify the impact of these psychological constraints.

In contrast to the above arguments or concerns about the recognition of public unions and subsequent collective negotiation, there are some real facts of public employment that require a basic attitudinal change among public employers and the general public. A good public administrator must realize that he is a public servant and represents the public interest. In a democratic government, he plays the role of a public servant whose principal concern is to serve people and not to govern his subordinates. The government managers as public employers ought to change their paternalistic and iron-handed policy toward public employees. Not only the creation of necessary laws but more affirmative action is needed to educate people, including public employees. Government as an employer is already competing with private industry and unless it improves its image among public employees, it is bound to face the odds in the near future. The reaction of public employees is reflected in a very sharp and critical statement by Jerry Wurf, president of the American Federation of State, County, and Municipal Employees (AFSCME):

Public workers are denied, with limited exception the minimum wage and overtime protections of the Fair Labor Standards Act; they are denied the protections afforded other workers under Title VII of the Civil Rights Act with respect to equal employment opportunities; they may be denied minimal health and safety protections under the Occupational Health and Safety Act; they are denied in many instances coverage under unemployment, workmen's compensation programs, and social security; they are prevented from exercising complete political freedom as citizens under the Hatch Act and similar statutes at the state and local government level; and they are denied the protections, rights and benefits afforded other workers under the National Labor Relations Act [Wurf, 1972: 25].

In addition to these arguments, John Macy (1972) states that there has been a general executive and legislative failure in the United States to take responsible care of its own employees. Such a failure has led to an increased appeal for union activity. The myth that public service employees deserve any less reward than those employees in the private sector has lingered much too long. Although increased union demand and the institution of bargaining may lead to a higher employee cost, the result in the long run should be greater productivity and better public service in general (in Zagoria, 1972: 14).

Edward Krinsky (1970) states that many governments have too long refused to accept that fact that public union activity is at hand, and have also refused to recognize the basic collective bargaining rights of the public sector employees. Perhaps the most important reason to recognize public unions and establish collective negotiation procedures in the public sector is the inevitability of strikes. If public workers are not afforded the right of union "recognition," the only recourse is to go on strike. In many areas, "recognition" is the major cause of strikes. The failure to provide public employees with organizational rights leaves them with no other alternative. State and municipal laws allowing public workers the right to organize and bargain collectively are the first steps to averting strikes and militant attitudes. If the necessary laws are not established to allow these employees to seek dignity at their work and a decent standard of living, the strike will always be the means the employees will utilize (Krinsky, 1970, 21: 464).

THE GROWTH OF PUBLIC EMPLOYEE UNIONS

The history of public union activity began in the early twentieth century with the formation of a number of small unions. As early as 1830, craft-type unions of "laborers, workmen, and mechanics" began to develop at both the federal and municipal levels. Also at about this time, the American Institute of Instruction, the predecessor of the National Education Association, was formed (Spero and Capozzola, 1973: 15). However, the first serious wave of municipal employee organization took place in the 1880s and 1890s with the formation of police and fire brotherhoods and fraternal organizations. These early organizations restricted their activities to only minor grievances in the prevailing political climate of the newly established "merit" system (Spero and Capozzola, 1973: 15-16). Many of the early twentieth century municipal union movements became closely affiliated with the municipal reform movement, in order to free employees from the manipulation of machine politics in such cities as New York and Chicago (O'Neill, 1970, 30: 1-2).

In 1918, the International Association of Fire Fighters was organized in the United States and Canada. It reached 180 chartered locals by 1919 and continued to grow in larger cities. In the early 1930s, public unionism began to take on a new shape with the organization of the AFSCME. This organization grew out of a small AFL chartered union known as the Wisconsin State Employees Association. The AFL had placed AFSCME under the control of the American Federation of Government Employees, an affiliate of the AFL whose members were mainly composed of federal employees. However, in 1936 the AFSCME under the leadership of Arnold Zander, was granted a separate charter (O'Neill, 1970, 30: 7-9).

The AFSCME is an all public union and its membership is composed only of employees serving in the public service. Another important aspect of public employee unionism represents mixed unions of which three are the most prominent:

(1) the Service Employees International Union (SEIU),
(2) the Laborers' International Union of North America (both affiliated with the AFL-CIO); and
(3) the International Brotherhood of Teamsters, Chauffers, Warehousemen, and Helpers of America.

These are all mixed unions because their members are drawn from private industry as well as from the public service. The SEIU in 1971 had a total estimated membership of 450,000, about one-third of whom were government employees. Of this one-third, 90 to 95 percent have been drawn from state and local governments. The SEIU has been competing vigorously with the AFSCME for public employees, yet its main strength lies in organizing workers employed in hospitals, schools, and social services in both state and local government agencies (Stieber, 1973: 3-4).

The Laborers' Union claimed a total membership of 550,000 in 1970, of which about 24,000 were state and local government employees. Its major membership gains started since 1963 when the union turned to public employment to offset a dwindling membership base. Although the union has tried to organized white-collar, and skilled craftsmen, its basic success has been the organization of sanitation, streets, and public works employees (Stieber, 1973: 4-5).

The Teamsters is the largest overall union in the United States. In 1970, its membership was about 57,000 public employees. Of these, four-fifths worked in municipal government with the rest divided equally among state, county, and school districts. The largest portion of the Teamsters public employees are involved in such activities as noninstructional educational service, public welfare, police protection, and parks and recreation. The Teamsters leadership is now putting on heavy pressure to obtain more public employee membership (Stieber, 1973: 5).

Among the uniformed protective services sector (that is, fire fighters and police), there is a great multiplicity and diversity of organizations. The Fraternal Order of Police had a membership of about 80,000 in 1969. Although its objectives are much similar to a "union," it does not associate itself with any union or "like organization." Unlike the FOP, the International Conference of Police Associations is a confederation of independent police associations. It now claims a membership of over 100 state and local associations with over 142,000 members. Police locals have also affiliated with the

AFSCME, SEIU, and Teamsters, as well as many local organizations unaffiliated with any larger organization.

In addition to all of these public organizations are state and local employee associations. While not actually unions, they offer low-cost insurance policies to employees on a group basis, lobby in state legislatures and city councils; some have even become full-fledged collective bargaining organizations. These associations differ in objectives and tactics from state to state, but all are against the formation of a national union. During the 1960s these associations registered a growth of 47 percent reflecting (as in public employee unions) the fact that public employees are organizing at a phenomenal rate. The combined 36 state employee associations claimed 618,000 members in 1969. Most of these associations are affiliated with a loose confederation known as the Assembly of Government Employees (AGE). Local associations of public employees, at this time, comprise around 300,000 members, concentrated mainly in California and the New York City area (Stieber, 1973: 5-9).

Professional associations have also experienced expansion in the past 10 years. Teachers constitute a major part of the National Education Association claiming over one million members in 1970, and the American Federation of Teachers with a membership of 165,000 (Cohany and Dewey, 1970: 17-18). The American Nurses Association is an organization of registered nurses that now has approximately 40,000 members in state and local employment. Setting up high professional standards and promoting economic interests are the two major objectives of this association (Stieber, 1973: 10-11).

Table 1 shows the breakdown of government employee membership in various employee organizations.

While not all inclusive, Table 1 shows that over three million public employees are now members of labor unions or associations. This figure is likely to go higher in the south and southwest, where unionization has not yet fully developed in the public service.

The fact that such growth has taken place must be taken as a sign that the public employee is beginning to realize his potential power and strength, through the utilization of organization.

Even so (as Table 2 indicates) union activity remains highest in the northeast and far west. The spread of unions into the south has just begun. Few mountain or southern states have laws or regulations to cope with public employee organizations as yet. It is quite likely that public unionism in the south and mountain states will enjoy major growth during the next 10 to 15 years. This is the section of the country that will soon desperately need legislation and regulations for managing union recognition and bargaining policies.

Table 2 indicates that the northern and eastern states have a much greater percentage of municipal unionized employees. While New England, the middle Atlantic, the Pacific, and the west north central states average well above 50 percent union representation, the Southern section and the Rocky Mountain states average around 30 percent representation.

TABLE 1
State and Local Government Employee Membership in Unions and Associations, 1969-1973

Organization	Membership in Thousands
Unions	
American Federation of State, County and Municipal Employees (AFSCME)	700[a]
International Association of Fire Fighters (IAFF)	160
Service Employees International Union (SEIU)	126
Laborers' International Union of North America	24
International Brotherhood of Teamsters	57
Others	50
Total: Unions	1,117
Association	
Fraternal Order of Police (FOP).	80
International Conference of Police Associations (ICPA)	142
State Associations	618
Local Associations	300
American Nurses Association (ANA)	40
National Education Association (NEA)	1,000[b]
American Federation of Teachers (AFT)	165[b]
Total: Associations	2,345
Total: Unions and Associations	3,462

Source: Stieber (1973: 2-12); a) 1974 figures (Time, July 1974: 41); b) 1970 figures: Cohany and Dewey (1970, 93: 17-18).

The southern and mountainous regions also have a much greater percentage of municipalities where no union representation occurs. The other sections of the country generally show increased representation by unions or associations up to around the 50 to 79 percent range.

Although the table does not contain recent data, it implies that the next targets for unionization are the southern and Rocky Mountain regions of the country.

LEGAL PARAMETERS

The first formal recognition of collective negotiation procedures took place in 1958, when Mayor Robert Wagner of New York City issued Executive Order No. 49. This order pledged to civil servants in New York City a labor relations program consistent "with the practices and procedures of collective bargaining prevailing in private labor relations." Although much of the recognition and bargaining was very informal and "crude" by modern standards, it was a very important step towards a goal of providing public employees with rights and privileges similar to private employees (Horton, 1973: 30-44).

TABLE 2

Number of Municipal Employees Represented by Unions or Associations by Geographic Region, 1968

Region	Total Cities	Employees		Percentage of Union Representation in Cities						
		Total	Percent Represented	No representation	1-24%	25-49%	50-79%	80-89%	90-99%	100%
New England	130	78,540	64	8%	17%	19%	36%	10%	8%	2%
Middle Atlantic	239	348,162	90	23%	11%	28%	18%	7%	6%	6%
East North Central	336	159,251	60	25%	10%	24%	27%	9%	4%	1%
West North Central	149	55,604	46	41%	17%	21%	15%	1%	3%	2%
South Atlantic	182	177,532	31	67%	14%	10%	7%	1%	1%	1%
East South Central	56	27,694	33	41%	23%	21%	11%	2%	2%	–
West South Central	135	70,272	26	60%	17%	16%	6%	–	1%	1%
Mountain	73	34,510	31	44%	25%	16%	8%	4%	–	3%
Pacific	230	159,261	64	19%	9%	13%	26%	13%	10%	10%

Source: Stieber (1973: 226).

National recognition in promoting public employee unionism at federal, state, and local levels was prompted by the issuance of Executive Order 10988 by President Kennedy in 1962. This order was preceded by E.O. 10987 which established the agency system for appeals from adverse actions. Both orders were issued following the recommendations of a task force report submitted to the president. The task force recommended that all federal employees should have the right to join employee organizations or to refrain from doing so. The E.O. 10988 set up three types of government recognition: formal, informal, and exclusive. Implementation was left up to each department head for the development of procedures for organization recognition, and determination of bargaining units, employee rights, and policies of consultation with employee representatives. Under the order, the U.S. Civil Service Commission was entrusted the task of developing a program to assist in carrying out the order (Roberts, 1970: 27-39).

Later in 1969, President Nixon issued Executive Order 11491 which greatly expanded the scope of 10988 order and made a number of changes. For example, under 11491, a special Federal Labor Relations Council was set up to administer the Order, prescribe regulations and make policy decisions. A Federal Services Impasses Panel was also created to assist parties in resolving negotiations (Roberts, 1970: 584-590).

Although some state and local jurisdictions had much earlier established employee organization policies and procedures for recognition, these orders at the federal level initiated a process of mass proliferation of laws and regulations in thousands of cities, counties, and in most states. Following the federal example, states began to develop wide range legislation. The various court decisions, executive orders, and attorney generals' opinions further strengthened the ability to deal effectively with problems of public labor-management relations (see Appendix).

PURPOSE AND SCOPE OF THE STUDY

The analytical scope of this paper covers legislative measures, executive orders, important court decisions and attorney generals' opinions. It does not include any discussion of contractual agreements agreed upon by a particular public agency and local employee union. With this background, the study focuses upon four important aspects of state policy regulations established to regulate public employer-employee relations:

(1) To examine the economic implications and service demands indicated by work stoppages.

(2) To suggest how best the remaining states, which do not have any formal laws to deal with public employee unions, can build around the experience gained by other states in establishing necessary laws.

(3) To present a comparative review of the nature and scope of existing state laws and policies established to conduct public employer-employee relations.

(4) To examine the regulatory norms and institutional structures and procedures established to implement various legislative measures.

Considering the growth of public employee unions or associations and their increased militancy, it is hard to believe that the pressure of union recognition or bargaining activities could be successfully contained, resisted, or managed without having necessary laws. If the main goal of public administration is to serve the public interest, it must keep "its own house in order." All of the theoretical arguments, or legal constraints for that matter, mean little in the face of a strike that can cripple a community.

Table 3 illustrates the seriousness of the problem created by public employee strikes. There is a tremendous waste of productive manpower hours, which has far-reaching economic consequences. Any strike by public employees also deprives people of certain essential services. We must remember at this point that 12.6 million people work in the public labor force, and of these, 77 percent are employed by state and local governments.

The strike or a threat to strike is a very strong weapon which the employee unions use to achieve their goals. Table 3 shows that with each passing year (in general) both the number of workers involved in stoppages and the number of man-days lost has increased dramatically at both the state and the local level. It may also be noticed that while the number of strikes between 1969 and 1970 appeared to level off, the number of workers involved and the number of days idle expanded greatly.

DETERMINANTS OF UNION RECOGNITION IN SOUTH

It is particularly interesting to note, as mentioned before, that unionization has just recently begun to develop in the southern states. Although there is little or no legislation relating to public employee relations in this section of the nation, there have been several strikes with significant impact on the delivery of public services. The public employee strikes in this region have not been concerned with better wages and working conditions, as is most often the case (Stenberg, 1972: 32, 102), but over union recognition. Table 4 illustrates this point and also indicates the need for public employee legislation in the South. Each of the strikes listed in the table was caused by the employees strong desire to seek union recognition by the local government.[2]

It is interesting tc note that most of the strikes in these southern cities were successful not only because of union backing and financial support, but because the strikers themselves had the determination to continue the strike until recognition was gained. In the case of Mobile, Alabama, the union could not get enough support to shut down the sanitation services. White

TABLE 3
Work Stoppages Among Government Employees, 1958-1970

	All Stoppages		
Year	No.	Workers Involved	Man–Days Idle
1958	15	1,720	7,510
1959	26	2,240	11,500
1960	36	28,600	58,400
1961	28	6,610	15,300
1962	28[a]	31,100	79,100
1963	29	4,840	15,400
1964	41	22,700	70,800
1965	42	11,900	146,000
1966	142	105,000	455,000
1967	181	132,000	1,250,000
1968	254[c]	201,800	2,545,000
1969	411[d]	160,000	745,700
1970	412[e]	333,500	2,023,200

State Government Employees			Local Government Employees		
No.	Workers Involved	Man–Days Idle	No.	Workers Involved	Man–Days Idle
1	30	60	14	1,690	7,450
4	410	1,650	22	1,830	9,850
3	970	1,170	33	27,600	57,200
–	–	–	28	6,610	15,300
2	1,660	2,260	21	25,300	43,100
2	280	2,160	27	4,560	13,300
4	280	3,170	37	22,500	67,700
–	–	1,280[b]	42	11,900	145,000
9	3,090	6,010	133	102,000	449,000
12	4,670	16,300	169	127,000	1,230,000
16	9,300	42,800	235	190,900	2,492,000
37	20,500	152,400	372	139,000	592,200
23	8,800	44,600	386	168,900	1,330,500

Sources: U.S. Bureau of Labor Statistics (1970: 9) and Stieber (1973: 160).

a Includes five stoppages of federal employees, affecting 4,190 workers and resulting in 33,800 man-days idleness.

b Idleness resulting from two stoppages beginning in 1964.

c Includes three stoppages of federal workers, affecting 1,680 workers resulting in 9,600 man-days idleness.

d Includes two federal stoppages affecting 600 workers and resulting in 1,100 man-days idleness.

e Includes three federal stoppages, affecting 155,800 workers and resulting in 648,300 man-hours idleness.

TABLE 4

**Public Employee Strikes and Determinants of Union
Recognition in the South, 1968-1970**

Place/Time	Outcome	Major Determinants of Success or Failure
Pascagoula, Mississippi: Department of Public Works and the AFSCME January 12 - 18, 1968	Successful	Major proportion of city's population was affiliated with the labor union. The size of labor population also insured the support of business community.
Memphis, Tennessee: Department of Public Works and the AFSCME February 12 - April 16, 1968	Successful	Major support given to strikers by the black community of Memphis, Racial overtones because of firing of 20 sewer workers, Mayor's attitude toward blacks (Negro Union) support by International (AFSCME)
Miami Beach, Florida: Department of Public Works and the AFSCME August 14 - 21, 1968	Successful	Characteristics of the city population 75% Jewish, 95% blacks composed sanitation workers, Heavy Reliance on Tourism, support of Dade Co. Federation of Labor.
Little Rock, Arkansas: Sanitation Workers and the AFSCME November 1 - 10, 1968	Successful	Firing of City Manager provided proper timing for the strikers. Sanitation workers were 75% black.
Madison County, Tennessee: Tennessee School Bus Drivers and County Highway Department Employees, and the AFSCME February 17 - 27, 1969	Successful	Strength of unionism in the community was Ladies Garment Union who also joined on picket lines, the impact of the Memphis Strike, the nature of the services affected.
Charleston, South Carolina: Medical College Employees and National Organizing Committee of Hospital Home Employees and the AFSCME March 20 - June 28, 1969	Successful	Racial overtones-12 black non-professionals were fired, HEW investigation findings, sensitivity of city: commercial base, Port workers support, UAW Support
Charlotte, North Carolina: Sanitation Employees and the AFSCME June 29 - August 5, 1969	Successful	Impact of school busing issue High Quality of union leadership and complete support of the black community and timing of the strike
Mobile, Alabama: Alabama Public Works Department and the Retail, Wholesale and Department Store Union June 17 - June 26, 1968	Unsuccessful	Union failed to shut down garbage service, Whites continued to work, Mayor immediately recruited replacement personnel, even some blacks came back to work.

TABLE 4 (Continued)

Place/Time	Outcome	Major Determinants of Success or Failure
Clayton County, Georgia: Georgia Waterworkers and the AFSCME April 3 - June 1, 1969	Unsuccessful	Political insulation of Waterworks Authority, very little support given to Strikers by their Union, change in Union leadership. No support from AFSCME.
Jackson, Mississippi: Sanitation Employees and the AFSCME June 29 - July 12, 1969	Unsuccessful	Inadequate financial support. Lack of support from the AFSCME

Source: Stepp (1974, 3: 59-69).

workers in the public works department continued to work, and the mayor simply replaced the striking personnel. In the cases of Clayton County, Georgia and Jackson, Mississippi the lack of support by unions was the major determinant in the failure of the strike and ultimate union recognition.

In many of the successful strikes, racial overtones were present, possibly indicating a major growth of unionism in the black membership of public employees. The growth of black union membership may provide major inroads for black public employees in the power structure, especially in municipal government, not only in the South but in all sections of the country.

It may also be implied from this spread of "recognition strikes" that these may begin to intensify with the passage of time unless political leadership in the South acts first with positive legislation and measures.

II. EXISTING STATE POLICIES AND LEGISLATION

In the past 10 to 15 years the area of public employee relations has seen a rash of laws, executive orders, and attorney generals' opinions concerning collective negotiations. Since the nature and scope of employee coverage differs in each state, the various states have been divided into three categories: progressive states, intermediate states, and primitive states. These three categories are determined on the basis of the type of bargaining rights afforded public employees as opposed to the type of rights currently enjoyed by employees in the private sector.[3]

For the purposes of analysis, states which have enacted laws that establish similar rights for the public employee, as compared to private sector, are termed "progressive states." States that at least allow or give the public employee a right to talk with the employer are termed as "intermediate" states. Finally those states which allow public employees to simply talk to the employer, have no laws at all, or have negative policy regulations are termed "primitive" states.

Because of constraints imposed by time and space, the study covers only major groups of public employees, which are broken down as:

(1) state employees,

(2) municipal employees,

(3) firemen,

(4) police, and

(5) teachers.

In some states, legislation has been directed at one specific group; wherever applicable, this will also be included.

THE PROGRESSIVE STATES

Based only upon the bargaining right granted in any state by some formal means (executive order, legislative measures, and so on), the states in the progressive category are those which require at least one group (such as police, fire, or teachers) to bargain collectively with their employers. Based upon this criterion the progressive states may be subdivided into three categories:

(1) state with mandatory collective bargaining statutes covering all public employee groups,

(2) those with laws covering most employee groups; and

(3) those with bargaining laws covering at least some groups.

For the sake of simplicity, these three groups can be referred to as high coverage, medium coverage, and low coverage respectively.

At the present time, 11 states have created laws that require collective bargaining between public employer and employee in all categories. These "high coverage" states are: Delaware, Hawaii, Massachusetts, Michigan, Minnesota, New Jersey, New York, Pensylvania, Rhode Island, Washington, and Wisconsin. These states have elected to cover all public employees in a variety of ways. Some states such as Hawaii, Massachusetts, Michigan, Minnesota, New Jersey, and New York have enacted one general statute covering all public employees, either by the passage of one general act or the amendment of a previous law over the years (U.S. Dept. of Labor, Summary, 1973: 2-37).

On the other hand, the state of Washington has chosen to cover different occupational groups at differing points in time. State employees were covered by a rule from the Washington State Personnel Board, local employees along with police and fire by statute passed in 1969, and teachers by still another statute enacted in 1965 (Washington State Personnel Board, Merit System Rules, 1965, 1967, 1969).

Regardless of the methods used, it is important to note that, in these 11 states, all public employees are required to bargain collectively.

Medium Coverage (Progressive)

Twelve states are listed in the medium category, meaning that these states do not require all public employees to bargain collectively, but they do require most employee groups to do so. These states are Alaska, Connecticut, District of Columbia, Florida, Maine, Nebraska, Nevada, New Hampshire, Oklahoma, Oregon, South Dakota, and Vermont.

The groups that are excluded from mandatory collective bargaining coverage vary from state to state. However, it is interesting to note that only Vermont excludes police from coverage (U.S. Dept. of Labor, Summary, 1973: 32). Only New Hampshire excludes local public employees from collective bargaining coverage. Most of the states chose, for one reason or another, to exclude either state employees, firemen, or teachers (U.S. Dept. of Labor, Summary, 1973: 2-32). Some states, Oregon for example, provide that localities may elect to have their employees covered under a mandatory collective bargaining agreement, on the basis of a general state law (Oregon, Revised Statute, Secs. 243.710-243.760 as amended by Senate Bill 55, 1969).

It seems reasonable to speculate that these states have excluded certain public employees from collective bargaining because of public management's own sense of priorities, or perhaps the groups excluded did not press for such rights. Nevertheless, the medium coverage states are certainly to be considered in the "progressive" category.

Low Coverage (Progressive)

Although it may be debatable whether these states may be considered in the progressive category, the fact remains that they have enacted legislation affecting collective bargaining for *some* public employee groups.

Idaho requires collective bargaining for teachers and firemen (Idaho Laws, Chap. 138, 1970 and Home Bill 209, 1971). Montana applies coverage to teachers and nurses (Montana Laws, House Bill 344, 1971 and Chap. 320 of 1969 Laws). Three states fall in this category by providing for manadatory collective bargaining, in the case of teachers in North Dakota and Maryland and firemen in Wyoming.

Two states that need to be mentioned as a sidelight in a "class of their own" are Kentucky and Georgia. Kentucky requires mandatory collective bargaining for firemen and policemen by saying it is the "authority and duty to bargain collectively." However, this statute applies only to counties of over 300,000 population and which have adopted the merit system (Kentucky Laws, House Bill 151, 1972 and House Bill 217, 1972).

In Georgia, firemen are under mandatory collective bargaining provisions provided their municipalities have a population of over 20,000 and they opt to be covered (Georgia Law, House Bill 569, 1971).

The "progressive category" as a whole includes 29 states plus the District of Columbia. Although for some of these states there is still a long way to go, a small beginning is better than nothing.

THE INTERMEDIATE STATES

Intermediate states have laws which are somewhat more restrictive on the rights of public employees. None of these states requires mandatory collective bargaining. These states belong to the intermediate category because there exists some legal basis for either

(1) requiring public employers and employees to "meet and confer" or,

(2) allowing, but not requiring, collective bargaining between employee and employer.

In these states there can be no negotiated collective agreement without the full agreement of government. In other words, government reserves the right to unilaterally determine all issues, but allows the employees the right of communication.

High Coverage (Intermediate)

In this category, are the three states which provide for mandatory "meet and confer" laws. These states are Kansas, California, and Missouri.

Kansas requires all of the five public employee groups to "meet and confer" with public employers (Kansas Laws, S.B. 333, 1971 as amended by S.B. 509, 1972). California provides mandatory "meet and confer" provisions for all public employees except firemen, while Missouri has similar statutes covering firemen, state and local workers (U.S. Dept. of Labor, Summary, 1973: 4-18).

The importance of mandatory meet and confer procedures lies in the fact that these procedures establish an institution whereby public employees may regularly air grievances. Such procedures are constructive in that they may overt trouble, and in that management is required to listen.

Medium and Low Coverage (Intermediate)

This category of intermediate states is reserved for that group which "is allowed to bargain collectively." As opposed to any mandatory requirements imposed upon either labor or management, these states simply have legal bases for collective bargaining agreements if "both employers and employees should agree to do so."

Within this group are seven states. Indiana provides "permissive" collective bargaining for all sectors of public employment as do Iowa and Utah (authority for Indiana: Atty. Gen. Opinion, August 8, 1969; for Iowa: State Board of Regents v. Packing Workers, 175 N.W. 2d 110, 1970; for Utah: Atty. Gen. Opinion, Oct. 1, 1945, and Jan. 12, 1960). Virginia provides for permissive collective bargaining for all but state workers through two Atty. Gen. Opinions of 1962 and 1970.

Illinois' provisions cover local public employees and teachers (Chicago Div. of Ill. Educ. Assn. v. Board of Educ. of City of Chicago, 222 N.E. 2d 243, 1966) while Arkansas provides for local and state employees (Atty. Gen. Opinion, Sept. 19, 1972).

New Mexico rounds out the intermediate states by permitting state workers to bargain collectively by the authority of the State Personnel Board in 1972.

In all, 10 states fall into the intermediate category, with the "high coverage" states differing markedly (by the legislation on the books) from the rest. It should be noted at this point, however, that states which have "permissive" collective bargaining may have many collective public employee agreements on record. However, the legislation that formally requires such negotiations or that institutionalizes formal employee-employer relations is lacking.

THE PRIMITIVE STATES

These states may be so labeled because of

(1) very restrictive public employee relations laws,

(2) negative laws, or

(3) no legislation in public sector relations at all.

The word "primitive" in this case connotes only the states restrictions upon public employees as opposed to private sector employers.

Included in this category are Alabama, Arizona, Colorado, Louisiana, Mississippi, North Carolina, South Carolina, Tennessee, Texas, and West Virginia.

Texas and Louisiana may be placed in the "high" category in this instance because these two states at least allow at least allow some public employees the right to present grievances to their employers. Texas recognizes the workers' right to organize and all public employees' right to present grievances (Atty. Gen. Opinion No. M-77, May 18, 1967). Texas law further states that it is against public policy for any governmental organization to enter into any collective bargaining agreement with any labor organization (Art. 514 E. Sec. 1, Laws of 1947).

Alabama gives firemen the right to present proposals to their employers (Title 37, Chap. 8, Art. 7, Sec. 450-3, Laws of 1967). However, by the Solomon Act (Act 720, Public Acts of 1953) Alabama prohibits public employees to join labor unions. If a person joins a labor union, or remains a member of a union should he already belong, the laws further state that he would lose all rights afforded him under the state merit system and all other rights or privileges afforded him as a result of his public employment.

Louisiana on the other hand, while not providing public employee bargaining rights to "major" employee groups, does requires (as of 1964) all public transportation systems to bargain collectively with their employees. This provision also provides compulsory arbitration in the event of impasse (Art. 127, Secs. 890 A & 890 E. appr. July 9, 1964).

North Carolina has enacted a law similar to Alabama's Solomon Act. North Carolina's law also forbids any public employee to join a trade or labor union. Violation of this law results in the commission of a misdemeanor which is punishable at the discretion of the court (Gen. St. of North Carolina, Secs. 95-100 and Art. 12).

The Arizona Constitution gives public employees the right to organize, but no other legislation has been forthcoming.

Colorado and Ohio, thus far, have no formal laws dealing with public employees. Mississippi and Tennessee have passed no laws, although some early court decisions have been of a "negative" nature. South Carolina, on the other hand—while not dealing with the right to organize or the right to collective bargaining—enacted two statutes creating grievance procedures for state and local employees (Goldberg, 1972: 64).

Table 5 presents a comparative perspective on all state laws and regulations dealing with bargaining rights of public employees. This table reflects what state governments have done in the area of recognition and establishment of bargaining rights. While many states have not recognized bargaining rights or public unions, where the unions have not been prohibited formally, negotiations may be actually carried out informally. The graphic projection presented in this section is only an indication of what states have done at the state level. It may not necessarily be a picture of reality at the municipal or county level.

It should be noted, however, that the clamor for passage of state laws in this field has grown in the past few years. The pressure for the enactment of formal state collective relations laws in the public sector has introduced a sharp rise in their passage. If passed by the state legislatures, the newly proposed legislative measures in Iowa, Florida, and Texas will consequently change the status of these states as projected in Table 5. Such change will affect particularly the type of employees covered and the nature of collective bargaining rights granted to them.

The trends shown in the following graphs are indicative of the remarkable gains made by public employee unions in the late sixties and especially the early seventies. Undoubtedly, as unions move into the as yet "unexposed" areas, the trend in passage of labor legislation will continue and intensify.

TABLE 5
Ranking of State Public Employee Relations Laws
Based on Bargaining Rights

PROGRESSIVE STATES

Governing Law,
Attorney Gen. Opinion
Court Decision
And Date

High

	State	Local	Police	Firemen	Teach.	Other
Delaware						
1970L	MCB	MCB	MCB	MCB		
1969L					MCB	
Hawaii						
1971L	MCB	MCB	MCB	MCB	MCB	
Massachusetts						
1965L	MCB					
1972L		MCB	MCB	MCB	MCB	
Michigan						
1965L	MCB	MCB	MCB	MCB	MCB	
Minnesota						
1972L	MCB	MCB	MCB	MCB	MCB	
New Jersey						
1968L	MCB	MCB	MCB	MCB	MCB	
New York						
1967L (amd)	MCB	MCB	MCB	MCB	MCB	
Pennsylvania						
1970L	MCB	MCB			MCB	
1968L			MCB	MCB		
Rhode Island						
1958L (amd.)	MCB	MCB				
1970L				MCB		
1970L			MCB			
1966L					MCB	
Washington						
1967 RPB	MCB					
1969L		MCB	MCB	MCB		
1965L					MCB	
1971L						MCB (Univ. System Teachers)
Wisconsin						
1971L	MCB					
1971L		MCB	MCB	MCB	MCB	

TABLE 5 (Continued)

Medium	State	Local	Police	Firemen	Teach.	Other
Alaska						
1972L	MCB	MCB	MCB	– –		
1972L					MCB	
Connecticut						
1969L	– –	MCB	MCB	MCB		
1969L					MCB	
Dist. of Col.						
1970 E.O.	N/A*	MCB	MCB	MCB	– –	
Florida						
1969C	– –	MCB				
1972L				MCB		
1969C			MCB			
1971L					MMC	
Maine						
1972L	– –	MCB	MCB	MCB	MCB	
Nebraska						
1972L	MCB	MCB	MCB	MCB		
1967L					PMC	
Nevada						
1971L	– –	MCB	MCB	MCB	MCB	
New Hampshire						
1969L	MCB	– –		– –	MCB	
1972L			MCB			
Oklahoma						
1972L	– –	MCB	MCB	– –		
1971L					MCB	
Oregon						
1969L	MCB	MCB	MCB	MCB		
1971L					MMC	
1969L						MCB (nurses)
South Dakota						
1970L (amd.)	MCB	MCB	MCB	– –	MCB	
Vermont						
1969L (amd.)	MCB					
1967L (amd.)		MCB	– –	MCB		
1969L					MCB	
Idaho						
1959A	– –	PCB	– –			
1970L				MCB		
1971L					MCB	
Montana						
1971L	– –	– –	– –	– –	MCB	
1969L						MCB (nurses)
North Dakota						
1951L	PCB	PCB	PCB	PCB		
1969L					MCB	

TABLE 5 (Continued)

Maryland 1969L	- -	- -	- -	- -	MCB	
Wyoming 1965L	- -	- -	- -	MCB	- -	
Georgia 1971L 1966A	- -	- -	- -	MCB	PCB	
Kentucky 1966PPS 1964A 1972[a] 1972[b] 1965A	PP	PP	MCB	MCB	PCB	

INTERMEDIATE STATES
High

	State	Local	Police	Firemen	Teach.	Other
Kansas 1972L 1970L	MMC	MMC	MMC	MMC	MMC	
California 1971 E.O. 1971L 1972L 1951L	MMC	MMC	MMC	PP	MMC	
Missouri 1969L 1968A	MMC	MMC	- -	MMC	PP	

Medium

	State	Local	Police	Firemen	Teach.	Other
Indiana 1972C	PCB	PCB	PCB	PCB	PCB	
Iowa 1970C	PCB	PCB	PCB	PCB	PCB	
Utah 1960A 1945A	PCB	PCB	PCB	PCB	PCB	
Virginia 1962A 1970A	- -	PCB	PCB	PCB	PCB	

Low

	State	Local	Police	Firemen	Teach.	Other
Illinois 1966C	- -	PCB	- -	- -	PCB	
Arkansas 1972A 1968C	PCB	PCB	- -	- -	- -	
New Mexico 1972 RPB	PCB	- -	- -	- -	- -	

TABLE 5 (Continued)

PRIMITIVE STATES
High

	State	Local	Police	Firemen	Teach.	Other
West Virginia 1962A	PP	PP	PP	PP	PP	
Texas 1967A 1947L	PP	PP	PP	PP	PP	
	Collective Bargaining is Against Public Policy					
Arizona Const.	RTO	RTO	RTO	RTO	RTO	
Louisiana 1964L	--	--	--			
1963L				RTO	RTO	MCB (transit worker)

Medium

	State	Local	Police	Firemen	Teach.	Other
Colorado 1961A	--	--	--	--	--	PCB (U. of Colo. workers)
Ohio	--	--	--	--	--	

Low

	State	Local	Police	Firemen	Teach.	Other
Mississippi 1946C			Policemen May Not Join Union			
South Carolina 1971L	GP	GP	--	--	--	
Tennessee 1958C			City May Forbid Employees to Belong to Unions			
Alabama 1967L	--	--	--	PP	--	
1953L		Public Employees May Not Belong to a Union				
North Carolina 1959L		Public Employees May Not Belong to a Union				

Sources: National Governors' Conference (1967: Passim); U.S. Department of Labor (1973: Passim) Summary of State Policy Regulations. Washington, D.C.: U.S. Government Printing Office.

L—Law
E—Executive Order
RPB—Role of Personnel Board
MCB—Mandatory Collective Bargaining
MMC—Manadatory Meet and Confer
RTO—Right to Organize
a & b—Law applies only to counties over 300,000, with merit system

C—Court Decision
L (amd.)—Laws as amended
PPS—Personnel Policy Statement
PCB—Permissive Collective Bargaining
PP—Right to Present Proposals
GP—Grievance Procedures
*N/A—Not Applicable

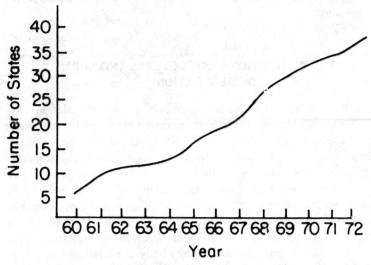

Number of States with Some Type of Formal Public
Employee Collective Relations Laws

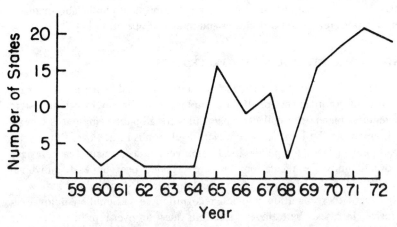

Number of Public Employee Collective Relations Laws
Passed Each Year Since 1959

The following section will deal with the institutions and procedures created in various states for the enforcement of laws relating to public sector employee relations.

III. THE INSTITUTIONAL STRUCTURES AND NORMS OF REGULATION

The methods of regulation and administration of employee relations laws will determine how effectively they have promoted better relations between the public employer and employees. Because of the current nature and the "experimental" type of these laws, methods of regulation appear quite similar among different states. However, as this section will show, laws differ in many respects across the nation. For example, laws and subsequent methods of regulation differ from state to state greatly depending upon the type of public employee group covered. Regulatory authority is given to an overall governing body, a newly created agency, or simply left with no regulation at all. Further, responsibility may rest with a state body or be assigned to a local body. Often the type of body varies according to the type of public employee group concerned. For instance, teachers are covered by a State Board of Education.

This section will point out some significant differences or similarities in the laws of different states concerning the procedures established by law for regulation, as well as administrative bodies set up for regulation and appeal procedures. While the factor of time precludes this analysis from being all-inclusive, it does examine some of the major aspects of public labor-management relations regulation procedures and modes of operation.[4]

INSTITUTIONAL STRUCTURES AND PROCEDURES

In **Alaska**, state law has provided for a state personnel board as the primary structure of enforcement for all state employees. As already mentioned, state law requires mandatory collective bargaining for all public employees excepting firemen. At the local level, however, regulation is turned over to the state department of labor for police, local employees, and firemen. Teachers have no overall body for regulation, but are presided over by each individual school board. Rules of procedure for regulation are also spelled out by law.

In regard to recognition policies, recognition for all public employees is exclusive. In cases where there is a serious question over representation, the appropriate administrative body—the state personnel board, the state labor department, or the school board—may conduct elections. Unit determination for the purpose of collective bargaining shall be decided again by the appropriate labor relations agency, excluding teachers. As far as regulations for impasse procedures are concerned, Alaskan law provides for compulsory mediation for most employee groups. Alaska has categorized public employees into three types: essential, semi-essential, and nonessential. These categories are based upon the employee's service provided to the community. Although this will be discussed somewhat later, compulsory arbitration is the method utilized by essential employee groups as an impasse procedure (Alaska Laws, 1972, chap. 113).

Teachers are also separated from other groups in the area of impasse regulation. According to Alaskan law a "mediation" board is created to issue findings and recommendations which are then made public. Actually the board serves basically a fact-finding function (Alaska Laws, 1970, chap. 18 as twice amended by laws of 1971 and 1972).

California, as opposed to Alaska, has elected to follow a "meet and confer" approach to employee relations. A number of patchwork laws have been enacted that seek to enforce procedures of public employee relations and bargaining. In this state, only police and local public employees are governed by some type of administrative body. For these two groups, the machinery of each governmental subdivision is responsible for regulation, if that subdivision elects to be covered under the law. No law relates to firemen in California, except a very old statute that allows them to present grievances (Calif. Labor Code, Secs. 1960-1963; and Calif. Laws of 1951, chap. 723). Recognition of employee groups differs from one group to another, both by type and procedure. For state employees, recognition is for union members only, and the employer bargains with unions for the time commensurate with membership. For local workers recognition is exclusive, if a majority of the members agree. The same applies for policemen. For teachers, however, recognition is proportional in that the employer will meet and confer with representatives of any employee organization through a certified employee council.

In the area of unit determination, only local workers and police are covered by law. Where problems arise, these two groups may ask for the assistance of the California state conciliation service. Impasse procedures in collective negotiation are also different for different groups. For state employees, a representative of the governor simply prepares a memorandum defining the areas of difference and the extent of such differences. This memorandum is available to the public. For the police and local employees, state law provides that they may agree to some form of mediation. Finally, the impasse procedure for state teachers is defined by law as any procedure which is mutually acceptable. If there is no such procedure, differences will be explored by a fact-finding body in efforts to make recommendations, which are non-binding (Calif. Laws: chap. 254, 1971, Chaps. 1964 of 1961 Laws and Secs. 3080-3089 of Edu. Code of 1970 as twice amended).

In **Connecticut**, state employees are not mentioned in the coverage of any employee relations law. However, local workers, police, and firemen are all covered under one general statute. This law created a state labor relations board with responsibility for developing modes and methods of regulation for all three groups. The law also stipulates these groups shall have exclusive recognition either through the chief municipal officer's recognition of the employee organization, or through elections conducted by the state board. Unit determinations are made exclusively by the state labor relations board. Impasse procedures consist of mediation by a special board of mediation, with a condition that all parties may petition for a fact-finding studies with non-binding recommendations (Conn. Gen. Statutes, P.A. 159 as amended by S.B. 406, and Conn. Laws of 1969).

Methods of regulation for teachers, however, include boards of education both at the state and local level. These boards grant exclusive recognition to majority representatives of employee groups, or if necessary, determine representatives through elections. If impasses develop, mediation is utilized by the state board of education unless either party requests advisory arbitration (Conn. Pub. Act 298, of laws of 1965, as once amended).

Delaware has followed similar procedures for state, local, police, and fire employees, with the institution of the state department of labor and industrial relations. Recognition procedures include exclusive recognition based upon SDLIR elections. This department further determines bargaining units, and excepts disputes over issues excluding those involving salaries, for mediation at the request of either party (Delaware Code, Chap. 13, Title 19, Secs. 1301-1313 as once amended). Similarly, Delaware has state and local boards of education that certify majority representatives, by election if necessary, and provide mediation in cases of impasse upon request of any party (Delaware Laws of 1969, chap. 40, Title 14)

The **District of Columbia** now has a board of labor relations that certifies majority representatives of employee groups in the areas of local, police, and firemen. The actual designation of majority representatives that gain exclusive recognition, however, is left to a personnel officer. The personnel officer also determines appropriate bargaining units in undisputed cases. The board of labor relations resolves impasses through the use of fact-finding procedures with final binding arbitration (E. O. 70-229 of June 1970). There are no provisions covering teachers.

Hawaii has instituted laws that create the Hawaii Public Employment Relations Board, which has responsibility for methods of regulation of all public employees. The PERB conducts elections among all employee organizations and certifies majority representatives with exclusive recognition. Unit determination for the purposes of bargaining are predetermined by existing law. Where controversy develops, however, the PERB intervenes. Should impasses develop during negotiations among any group of public employees and their employers, the PERB may appoint mediation and fact-finding boards, or the parties may agree to binding arbitration. Hawaii's far-reaching statutes further provide that willful interference into impasse procedures will be a misdemeanor (Hawaii Laws of 1970, Act 191, as twice amended).

The state of **Kansas** has recently enacted statutes that conform remarkably well to the Hawaii model, except that Kansas has followed a "meet and confer" approach. Kansas has also developed a state public employee relations board, with responsibility for all public employees except teachers. The PERB grants exclusive recognition to employee groups after it conducts elections, and further determines appropriate bargaining units. In cases of negotiation impasse, the board may institute either mediation, fact-finding with recommendations, or voluntary arbitration (Kansas Laws of 1971, S.B. 333, as once amended).

As in many other states, teachers in Kansas are covered by the state board of education which grants exclusive recognition to employee groups and determines appropriate bargaining units (Kansas Laws of 1970, H.B. 1646). However, no provision is made for impasse procedures.

In **Maine**, the state employees appeal board was created to mediate all grievances and disputes of state employees except those concerning classification and compensation procedures. The decision of this body is binding. In regard to all other public employees, however, a different procedure has been worked out. First of all, a public employee labor relations board was created. For the purposes of employee group recognition, the employer grants exclusive recognition upon satisfactory evidence of majority support. If a majority is in doubt, however, the executive director of the PELRB conducts elections to determine majority representatives. Any party that does not agree with his determination may appeal to the PELRB. Decisions from this board are then appealable to an appropriate superior court. A similar appeals process is also applicable in the area of bargaining unit determination. Should impasses in negotiations develop, the parties to the dispute may upon joint agreement institute mediation or fact-finding procedures. There are also provisions for voluntary binding arbitration (Laws of Maine, chap. 9A, 1969, as twice amended).

In Massachusetts, Michigan, and Minnesota, the institutions and procedures of regulation are surprisingly similar. **Massachusetts** has created a state labor relations commission, that covers all public employees. The SLRC grants exclusive recognition to majority representatives of employee groups, and is solely responsible for the determination of bargaining units for the purposes of negotiation. In case of impasse, Massachusetts law provides that the director of personnel and standardization should institute fact-finding procedures with non-binding recommendations. However, the fact-finder, once involved in a dispute, is not precluded from utilizing mediation to help resolve the impasse (Massachusetts Laws of 1965, chap. 149, as twice amended).

Michigan's employment relations commission performs similar duties to that of Massachusetts board. However, in the case of impasse in negotiation, mediation and fact-finding with non-binding recommendations are utilized in noneconomic issues. For economic issues the methods of compulsory, binding, final offer arbitration are utilized. The MERC covers all public employees in the entire state (Michigan H.B. 2953, Laws of 1965).

Minnesota has created detailed procedures for regulation of all public employee relations. By a 1971 law, this state created both a Minnesota public employment relations board and bureau of mediation services headed by a director. The director of mediation services certifies employee organizations with exclusive recognition upon a proper showing. Should there be some confusion over this point, the director may conduct an election. The director of mediation services is also responsible for determining appropriate bargaining units. These decisions may be appealed to the MPERB.

Mediation is utilized in the case of impasse. However, in the case of mediation failure, the MPERB must initiate final offer arbitration which is binding upon the employee organization only. The public employer is given 10 days to reject the decision of the MPERB. However, for nonessential employees the decision is binding upon the parties by request. For essential employees, the final decision is binding upon both parties (Minnesota S.B. N. 4, Laws of 1971).

In **Missouri**, a state board of mediation was created to regulate employee relations for state workers, local workers, and firemen. Exclusive recognition is once again the rule. The board resolves issues of majority status, and its determination may be appealed to a circuit court. The same procedure is utilized in the determination of bargaining units. In the case of impasse, however, mediation is utilized only in the case of local employees and firemen (Missouri H.B. No. 166, laws of 1967, as once amended).

In **Montana**, only two groups of employees are required to bargain collectively: teachers and nurses. Control of employee relations is left up to local school boards and the state board of health. Recognition is exclusive with the school board and the SBH is responsible for determining majority representatives. In the determination of bargaining units, it is expected (in the case of nurses) that both parties should be in agreement upon these questions. If they cannot reach agreement, the SBH determines the appropriate unit. Although there are no established impasse procedures for nurses, an impasse panel is created in the case of dispute concerning teacher negotiation. Each party in the negotiation chooses one member of the panel, while a senior district judge selects the third and final member. The panel then sets out on a fact-finding mission in order to make recommendations that are made public (Montana H.B. No. 455, laws of 1971 and chap. 320, laws of 1969).

In **Nebraska**, all public workers are covered by a court of industrial relations which applies exclusive recognition to all majority representatives of employee organizations as well as determining the appropriate bargaining unit. In the case of impasse in negotiation, the CIR may make available mediators and fact-finders. The jurisdiction of the CIR may be invoked through the request of the parties involved, the state attorney general, or by order of the governor. After such an imposition, the CIR may change wages, hours, and working conditions of the public employees. Such decisions are binding on all parties (Nebraska laws of 1947, chap. 178, as twice amended in 1969 and 1972).

Teachers in the state are under the direction of local school boards who must determine majority representatives for exclusive recognition. In the case of impasse, ad hoc fact-finding boards may be established for the purpose of arriving at recommendations that are non-binding. Once all of these procedures are exhausted, with unsatisfactory solutions, the CIR may step in (Nebrasksa H.B. 485, laws of 1967).

In **Nevada**, all public workers except state workers have collective bargaining rights. One law created the local government employee management relations board to regulate employee relations. In this state the local employer grants exclusive recognition to employee organizations provided that they have taken an oath not to strike. In cases of dispute the board rules, or conducts elections, to determine majority representatives. Similar procedures are used for bargaining unit determination. Impasse procedures include mediation by agreement of both parties or fact-finding. In Nevada the governor has the authority to institute fact-finding with recommendations to be binding on all parties (Nevada Laws of 1969, chap. 650, as once amended).

In **New Hampshire** a 1969 law extended the right to bargain collectively to state employees, policemen, and teachers. The law further created the management employee relations commission that grants exclusive recognition and determines bargaining units in the case of state employee organizations. In the case of police and teachers, exclusive recognition occurs on the basis of voluntary recognition. In cases of dispute, the city clerk conducts employee elections. Impasse procedures for state employees include provisions for parties to establish their own procedures for mediation or fact-finding. For teachers and police these procedures include mediation and fact-finding with written reports to be made public (New Hampshire State Code, chap. 98C of the laws of 1969).

New Jersey created a public employment relations commission in charge of supervising employee relations for all public employees. It is in charge of granting exclusive recognition and determining the appropriate bargaining units. Most impasse disputes are resolved through mediation, or the PERC may invoke fact-finding or arbitration (New Jersey Employer-Employee Relations Act, as once amended by chap. 303, laws of 1968).

New York has developed a public employment relations board, and a set of procedures for all public employees. Recognition and unit determination procedures closely follow those of New Jersey. However, in the area of impasse procedures there is a great difference. In New York, the PERB provides mediators and/or fact-finding boards upon either party's request or upon its own initiative. If fact-finding recommendations do not find acceptance, the state legislature or one of its committees makes a final decision to resolve the dispute (New York Laws of 1967, chap. 392, as four times amended).

Oklahoma has also established a public employee relations board to cover local workers, firemen, and police. Procedures for recognition include exclusive representation as determined by corporate authorities. The board settles disputes that may arise in this area. Advisory arbitration is provided in the case of impasse, which is binding upon the bargaining agent if it is adopted by the corporate authorities (Oklahoma State S.B. 105, laws of 1971, as once amended).

Teachers are treated separately, however, as they are supervised by local school boards, who determine majority representatives for exclusive recognition and create ad hoc fact-finding committees to resolve negotiation disputes (Oklahoma H.B. 1325, laws of 1971).

Oregon too has followed the lead of most states with the creation of a public employee relations board at the state level to cover state, local, police, and fire employees. Exclusive recognition is granted on the basis of procedures established by local jurisdictions or through PERB determination. In bargaining unit determination, the PERB decides for state employees; local jurisdictions may establish their own procedures or defer to the board. Impasse procedures include conciliation, mediation, fact-finding, or voluntary arbitration (Oregon Rev. Statutes, Secs. 342.450-342.470, as twice amended; and Oregon H. B. 1360, laws of 196a, as once amended).

Pennsylvania enacted a comprehensive law covering all employees in 1970. The law created the Pennsylvania labor relations board which conducts elections among employees to determine exclusive recognition, and also determines appropriate bargaining units. Disputes in negotiations are resolved either through the Pennsylvania bureau of mediation or fact-finding panels appointed by the PLRB. Otherwise parties may agree to arbitration. Firemen, however, are subject to complusory binding arbitration (Pennsylvania S.B. 1333, laws of 1970).

South Dakota has also passed laws for a state labor and management relations board under the direction of a commissioner. The commissioner determines exclusive recognition through elections and determines bargaining units. South Dakota law simply states that the commissioner may take whatever steps are necessary to resolve impasses in negotiations. In the case of firemen, however, recognition questions are decided through a vote of the members of each department. In the case of impasse, the state labor commissioner appoints a fair hearing board for binding arbitration. Its decisions are appealable to the appropriate circuit court (South Dakota laws of 1970, chaps. 3-18 as revised and amended; and South Dakota S.B. 121, laws of 1971).

Vermont's public employee laws cover all employees except policemen. Like most states, Vermont too created a state employee labor relations board which grants exclusive recognition to representatives receiving at least 51 percent of an election vote. The SELRB also determines the appropriate bargaining unit, and such decisions are appealable to the state supreme court. Impasse procedures for state employees include fact-finding panels which supply recommendations that are not binding. In the case of local employees, the commissioner of labor and industry appoints a mediator, or a third fact-finder, if necessary. Recommendations are then made public (Vermont laws of 1969, chap. 27 as once amended; and Vermont Pub. Act No. 198, laws of 1967 as once amended). Teachers are subject to a different law, under the administrative control of every local school board.

Washington has given a state personnel board the responsibility of certifying exclusive bargaining representatives and bargaining units for all state employees. Impasse procedures for state workers include submission of the issue to the director of personnel with a final hearing by the personnel board (Washington State Pers. Board, Merit System Ruled, chap. 356.32, 1967).

For local employees, police, and firemen, a special state department of labor and industries was created to conduct "recognition" elections and determine units. It also provides for a special mediation service in the SDLI for the resolution of negotiation disputes (Washington laws of 1969, chap. 108, secs. 41.5600.41-41.56.900 as once amended). Teachers and state university system educators are subject to different laws and procedures.

Wisconsin established the Wisconsin employee relations commission in 1966. Its duties are similar to those of other states' administrative bodies in funciton. The WERC grants exclusive recognition to majority employee representatives, but state-wide statutes determine bargaining units for state employees. Bargaining units are distinguished by the WERC for all other employee groups.

For state and local employees, in case of disputes in negotiation, the WERC appoints mediators, or investigates to determine whether fact-finding should be initiated. This also applies to teachers.

However, impasse procedures for police and firemen are markedly different. In this instance, the WERC appoints a mediator, or there is a final and binding arbitration. Arbitration is the "final offer" type unless otherwise agreed upon by parties to the dispute (Wisconsin laws of 1966, sub-chap. V of chap. III, as once amended, and laws of 1959, sub-chap. IV, chapter II, section 111.70).

CENTRALIZATION v. DECENTRALIZATION

The foregoing analysis of state laws suggests that in dealing with the administration of public labor laws, the states have chosen different methods for enforcing these laws. In general, states with more recent statutes have chosen a more progressive stance with regard to comprehensive coverage. For example, these states have enacted laws to cover *every* employee, and in general have assigned all enforcement and regulatory activities to a single administrative body functioning at the state level. In most cases, the agency responsibilities include determination of bargaining units for negotiation, and developing procedures for resolving impasses that may develop during negotiation. Furthermore, the body, according to the statute in effect, may or may not initiate procedures of recognition. However, the important point is that in the past five years many states have gone to this "comprehensive type" of approach. This type of approach has as its central tenet a "centralized" form of regulation for all workers—that is, responsibility for regulation rests with one administrative body.

Conversely, there have been some other states (such as Connecticut, Oklahoma, North Dakota, and Montana) that have preferred a "decentralized approach" to regulation. Whereas their laws may apply to all of the major public employee groups, some groups are covered by a separate law that provides for that group to be regulated and certified by a separate administrative body. In most cases, this administrative body may be at the local level—the local school board and school district are the best examples. Furthermore, statewide bodies may exist for local workers, police, firemen, and so on. The general theory behind this approach lies not necessarily in the area of decentralized control, perhaps as much as it does in specialized control. In other words, it is felt that special boards are better able to understand and communicate with employee groups in their field, on a like basis. School boards at the local level are better able to understand the needs and concerns of teachers in that area. A state personnel board is more likely better able to understand the needs of state public employees, and so on. There is no real method of evaluating these two types of employee relations regulation procedures. Some variables in the political climate of one state may be relevant in one state and are not characterized by same degree of emphasis in other state. Obviously, the type of regulation adopted in any one state reflects the concerns, values, and attitudes of the individual legislators in that state. Whether the legislature opts for a centralized approach or a decentralized approach depends mainly on the polarization or depolarization of political forces and the attitude of individual legislators and politico-administrative forces towards public employee unions.

So far this discussion has dealt with states in which regulatory procedures or enabling legislation covers all major public employee groups. A number of states such as California, Missouri, Rhode Island and Vermont have enacted laws in a patchwork fashion, that is, in a given state, one law covers some but not all employees, or a number of laws each apply to only one employee group. For a number of reasons, such states have chosen to exclude one or more groups from legislation, or have designed legislation specifically to fit one employee group. In a state which enacts overall regulatory legislation, yet excludes perhaps one employee group from that legislation, there can be a great deal of speculation as to why. Perhaps the state feels that a certain group renders an essential public service, and should not be included in the law because it would be a first step in organizing that group that may subsequently use the strike. Such states would obviously be hesitant to give collective bargaining rights to firemen or policemen.

In other areas, the fear or employee militancy in certain groups, or militancy and political punch, forced state legislatures to include essential groups within these laws. Perhaps the motivation here lies in the assumption that by creating regulatory procedures and establishing negotiation channels, the possibilities of strikes by employees rendering essential public services can be substantially lessened. As a result these states have sought to include these groups or one of them at least, in its employee relations law, in a positive manner.

Then, of course, there is always the variable of political support both on the part of lobbying groups and on the pressure the employee group itself is willing to exert (politically, not necessarily through an employee strike). In many states, undoubtedly, many employee groups just did not have enough political support in the legislative body, or the group itself did not want or care to be covered under employee relations laws. In some cases, both factors may be combined to produce legislative "inaction" while in others only one factor is strong enough to block action. The factors of political support for public employee relations laws for any particular group, and the pressure that group itself is willing to exert are major reasons for the inclusion or exclusion of a given employee group from public labor-management relations laws.

Procedures for appropriate unit determination are fairly uniform from state to state. Most states provide for the administrative body to either designate the units, or settle disputes over unit determination.

Impasse procedures also, are fairly uniform. Most states provide for fact-finding panels with recommendations combined further with some form of mediation. Arbitration of a binding nature, when used, is usually only for special employee groups that fall into the category of "essential" workers.

The next section will delve further into procedures and norms of regulation as well as explore some of problems experienced in the implementation of public employee relations laws in various states.

IV. OPERATIONAL DIMENSIONS OF PUBLIC EMPLOYEE LAWS

The management of men participating in an organizational setting involves a complex set of interacting relationships and influences. An ordering of systematic conduct of such relationships requires a governing force of laws and procedures. In the assessment of any public law, the impact has to be judged in terms of institutional capabilities, effective procedures, and policy controls. In the case of public labor management relations laws, the art of managing or enforcing affects various phases of public employer-employee relationships. Broadly, the analysis presented in this section will center around policies of different states as they relate to strikes, the scope of collective bargaining in negotiation, provisions defining unfair labor practices, union security practices, and administration of agreements. For the sake of clarity, each of these areas has been defined and dealt with separately.

RIGHT TO STRIKE POLICIES

A strike may be defined as a:

temporary stoppage of work of a concerted withdrawal from work by a group of employees of one establishment or several establishments, to express a grievance or to enforce demands affecting wages, hours, and/or working conditions [Roberts, 1970: 18].

At this time, by law or some other form of regulation, 39 states have outlawed strikes by public employees. This is not to say that strikes do not occur in public employment; they do, as has already been discussed in proceeding sections of this study.

Generally, with regard to strike policies, states may be divided into three categories:

(1) states having total prohibition on strikes by public employees,

(2) states granting public employees a limited right to strike; and

(3) states having no provision affirming or denying public employees the right to strike.

Starting with the first group, a majority of the states fall in this category. They have banned public employees from striking. In most cases, regulatory norms are prescribed by formal laws. However, in some cases they are simply governed by court decisions or attorney generals' opinions. This category includes states with some type of regulation that may apply to any class or group of public employees. Some states have prohibited the strike formally, for only a few groups of employees. Because of the different types of procedures and enforcement methods in each state, it would be more advantageous to list the states with provisions, one by one:

Alabama—Bans the strike totally for all public employees (Alabama Atty. Gen. opinion, 1957).

Arkansas—By attorney general's opinion has outlawed the strike for all state employees. Other public employees are not covered by any antistrike regulation (Arkansas Atty. Gen. opinion, 1968).

California—Has banned the strike for firemen, police, and local workers only. There are no provisions that apply to state workers or to teachers (San Diego v. AFSCME Local 127, 87 Calif. Reporter 258).

Connecticut—Has outlawed the strike for all public employees, through a court decision as well as by state statute (Norwalk Teachers Assoc. v. Norwalk Board of Education, 83A, 2nd 482; Connecticut Gen. statutes, Public Act 159, 1965).

Delaware—Has also declared strikes by public employees to be illegal for all workers. Strikes by teachers, however, can result in the loss of exclusive representative status for two years, and the laws of a "dues check-off" for one year (Delaware Code, chap. 13, title 19, secs. 1301-1313; Delaware Laws of 1969, chap. 40, title 14).

District of Columbia—Forbids strikes by any public employee (E.O. No. 70-229).

Florida—The strike is expressly forbidden to all public employees. In the case of teachers, the prohibition clause must be stipulated in the contract agreement (Florida Statutes Annotated Chap. 839, (1959); Dade County Classroom Teachers' Assoc. v. Rayan 225 So. 2nd 903, 1969; Florida Laws of 1971, chaps. 71-686).

Georgia—Has regulations now in effect that ban the strike for state workers, firemen, and teachers. State employees, if these provisions are violated, may suffer termination of employment, loss of civil service status, and re-employment may be banned for three years (Code of Georgia Ann., chap. 89-13, secs. 89-1301 and 89-1304).

Illinois—All strikes by all public employees are illegal (Board of Education of Community Unit School District No. 2 v. Doris Reading, 207 N.E. 2nd 427).

Indiana—All strikes are illegal (Anderson Federation of Teachers v. School, City of Anderson, 254 N.E. 2nd 329).

Iowa—All strikes by all public employees are illegal (State Board of Regents v. Packing House Workers, 175 N.W. 2nd 110).

Kansas—Forbids all strikes by all groups of public employees. According to Kansas law, strikes are defined as an unfair labor practice (Kansas Law of 1971, S.B. 333).

Kentucky—Forbids all strikes for all employees, except state workers, who are not covered by any regulation (Jefferson Co. Teachers Assoc. v. Board of Education, 75 LRRM 2486).

Maine—Strikes are forbidden as an unfair labor practice to all public employees except state workers (Maine Laws of 1969, chap. 9-A).

Maryland—Strikes are probhited only for teachers, who may lose the right of exclusive representation status for two years and the loss "dues check-off" for one year (Maryland Laws of 1969, sec. 160, sec. 160, chap. 405).

Massachusetts—The 1965 Massachusetts law that created the state labor relations commission also prohibited the strike by all public employees, defining it as an unfair labor practice.

Michigan—By a court decision, Michigan has outlawed the use of strikes for all public employees (Holland School District v. Holland Education Assoc., 157 N.W. 2nd 206).

Minnesota—In its new 1972 labor relations law it has banned the strike for all public employees. Strikers may be subject to an automatic termination of employment, or no compensation increase for one year and possibly probationary status for two years. An appropriate court may be appealed to for review in the case of disputes.

Missouri—Its 1967 employee relations law has prohibited the use of the strike by state workers, local workers, and firemen. No provisions are made requiring police and teachers.

Montana—Prohibits strikes by teachers as an unfair labor practice. Violation of the provision may result in suspension without pay, or dismissal, plus the loss of salary for each day of the duration of the strike (Montana Laws of 1971, H.B. 455).

Nebraska—Prohibits strikes by all public employees. Violation of this provision may result in fines and/or imprisonment for not more than one year (Nebraska Laws of 1947, chap. 178).

Nevada—Prohibits strikes by all public workers excluding state employees. Violators may be punished by fines up to $50,000. Officers of the employee organization may be punished by fines up to $1,000 per day and/or possible incarceration. Strikers may be dismissed or suspended (Nevada Laws of 1969, chap. 650).

New Hampshire—Prohibits strikes by state workers, police, and teachers. A bargaining agreement must contain strike prohibitions in the document itself. Violations of the regulation may result in decertification of the exclusive bargaining representative, and strikers will be subject to the penalties of law and regulations governing personnel misconduct (New Hampshire State Code, chap. 98C).

New Jersey—Prohibits strikes by all public employees (Board of Education v. New Jersey Education Association, 69 LRRM 2870).

New Mexico—Prohibits strikes by state workers only (New Mexico Personnel Board Regulations).

New York—New York's public employee relations law of 1967 prohibits the use of the strike for all public employees. Enforcement measures include placing strikers on probation for one year without tenure, as well as deducting an amount of twice the daily pay of the individual, for each day of the strike. Employee organizations lose all rights to exclusive representation dues check-off privileges as determined by the public employee relations board. The same board may impose fines and penalties, which are enforceable through the state supreme court.

North Dakota—Prohibits strikes by all public employees except state workers (City of Minot v. Teamsters Local 74, 142 N.W. 2nd 612).

Ohio—Prohibits strikes by all public employees. Strikers may have their employment terminated at the onset of a strike. However, the employee may be rehired later, with no pay increase for one year, or may serve a two year probationary period without tenure (Ferguson Act, Page's Ohio Revised Code, 1947, title 41, chap. 4117, secs. 4117.01-4117.05).

Oklahoma—In its 1971 public employee relations law, forbids strikes for all public employees. Negotiated agreements must contain the strike disavowal. Fines and/or imprisonment may be utilized as punishment in the event of violation.

Oregon—In its 1969 law, prohibits all public employees excluding teachers from the right to strike.

Rhode Island—The right to strike is forbidden to all public employees.

South Carolina—The strike is forbidden to all public employees (South Carolina, atty. gen. opinion no. 1778, 1964).

South Dakota—Prohibits the strike to all public employees except firemen in its 1970 employee relations law. Penalties against the striking organization are set by courts, with a maximum of $50,000 fine and/or imprisonment of the officials for one year. Strikers may be subjected to a fine of $1,000 and one year imprisonment. Employees do have the right of review by a court.

Tennessee—Strikes by all public employees are prohibited (City of Alcoa v. IBEW, 203 Tennessee 12; 308 S.W. 2nd 476).

Texas—Strikes are prohibited for all public employees (Texas, atty. gen. opinion no. M-77, 1967).

Vermont—Strikes are prohibited for all public employees. For local employees, the strike is prohibited only after the strike is determined to endanger health, safety, or welfare of the public. This policy also applies to firemen and police (Vermont Laws of 1967, Act No. 198).

Virginia—All strikes are prohibited by law (Code of Virginia 1950, title 40, secs. 40-65 to 40-67). Strikers are automatically fired and are not subject to reemployment for at least one year.

Washington—Strikes on the part of all public employees except teachers are illegal.

Wisconsin—All strikes by any public employee group or organization are illegal.

The foregoing analysis of strike policies reflects great fear among most state officials of the use of the strike by public employees. The tough enforcement provisions of many statutes now in effect are designed to deter public unions and organizations for even considering the strike as a viable alternative. Yet, these laws have not been as effective as they were intended to be. Public employees have continued to use the strike to achieve their ends.

Often times, once an areas is hit by a public strike, the nature of the service lost to the public is one of such a vital nature that most public officials entertain the strikers' demands and allow them to come back to work with no penalty. The duration of the strike and the type of service affected may often preclude the imposition of punishment upon the striking party.

As a result, many laws and regulations prohibiting strikes and also providing serious punishments for violators do not serve their intended purposes. They do not conform to reality in many cases, because they cannot measure the influence of political forces that affect strike in any given situation. What may lead employees to strike is likely to have little bearing on the deterrent nature of these laws. Employee organizations know that if they can get the support they require, and apply the necessary amount of pressure, they can get their demands fulfilled and suffer little, if any, for violating any provisions. The willingness and readiness to utilize the strike, in many cases, is not affected by the tone of the law.

In the second category, three states provide employees with a limited right to strike. These states are Alaska, Hawaii, and Pennsylvania. Alaska has classified its public employees into three categories: essential, semi-essential, and nonessential. These categories are based upon the nature of the services offered to the public. Essential workers are prohibited from striking. There is a "limited" right to strike for semi-essential employees, and nonessential are given the right to strike. These provisions were enacted as part of Alaska's overall employee relations act in 1972.

In Hawaii, all employees are granted a limited right to strike. However, employee strikes that may endanger the health and safety of the public are illegal. This determination is made by the public employee relations board, which also may petition a court for an injunction against an illegal strike. These procedures were provided for in Hawaii's act of 1970.

All public employees in Pennsylvania are subject to a limited right to strike, excluding firemen. This right is granted unless or until the strike presents a "clear and present danger" to the health, welfare, or safety of the public. A court must make such a determination. These procedures are part of Pennsylvania's 1970 employee relations law.

Finally, nine states have no formal policies, as they relate to strikes by public employees. These states are: Arizona, Colorado, Idaho, Louisiana, Mississippi, North Carolina, Utah, West Virginia, and Wyoming.[5]

SCOPE OF BARGAINING IN NEGOTIATIONS

The scope of bargaining refers to the limits, boundaries, and dimensions of issues and topics discussed during the stage of formal collective bargaining negotiations. In the public service, this problem is one of a great magnitude, since "policy" matters (matters dealing with the legal acts and policies of the state and subsequently the public) are often confused with personnel matters. Where collective bargaining has been adopted in public employment, the scope of bargaining has normally been limited by statute and procedures.

As in the private sector, it is often related to wages, hours, and conditions of employment.

It is widely recognized that policy issues should be excluded from bargaining issues. It is felt that bargaining issues should not undermine management's decision-making responsibility or authority. The scope of bargaining arrangements is also important in that bargaining issues, it is felt, need to be distinguished from issues that impinge upon merit regulations—such as tenure, promotion, and classification. Although the question of the effect of collective bargaining in the public service upon the merit system will be discussed latter, the problems of defining a proper "scope" of issues in negotiation as opposed to merit issues are important to identify here. Most states, nevertheless, have attempted to define the boundaries of negotiation through legal statutes. Because of limitation of time and space the following discussion will limit itself to the type of procedures that are followed in contract management in a given state.

In almost all of the states with collective negotiation laws and procedures, the scope of bargaining in negotiation is defined by the statutes as "wages, hours, and other conditions of employment." From state to state, the semantics may change but the meaning and practice across the nation represent the same spirit. Many laws include such items as grievances procedures, leave policies, fringe benefits, and vacations. The inclusion of such items in the law itself may serve little purpose since "conditions of employment" is a rather large catch-all device.

It is interesting to note that in a majority of states teachers enjoy a much greater "scope" of bargaining. In many states, the bargaining issues for teachers include those matters which relate to professional standards and school policies themselves. Obviously, the reason the scope of issues is wider for teachers is due largely to the differences in the nature of responsibilities between teachers and other public employees.

A few states have chosen to include some other items within the scope of bargaining for some public employees, however. For example, in Vermont the law states that not only does the scope of bargaining include pay, terms and conditions of employment, but also any matter mutually agreed upon by the negotiating parties. Theoretically, at least, the door is open to discuss any issue.

In Washington, the scope of bargaining (for state employees) includes all matters, but the appointing authority (the agency) may exercise discretion. Again the scope appears rather wide. However, it must be remembered in both of these instances that management will exercise the controlling option over what will and will not be discussed. It would be naive to assume that the management side of the table would agree to discuss areas which border or impinge upon its own authority or integrity.

Only a few states, such as Hawaii, have excluded issues (by law) normally dealt with by a state civil service commission. This is not to imply that most states allow negotiations in collective bargaining to supersede the authority of the state civil service commission. Such a case may occur, but is probably rare. Provisions defining the scope of bargaining are distinguished more by their striking similarities than their appreciable differences.

THE ADMINISTRATION OF COLLECTIVE BARGAINING AGREEMENTS

The collective bargaining agreement, as it emerges from the negotiating process, is a mutually agreed upon set of rules that have been jointly developed to guide employer-employee relationships for a fixed period of time. Generally, collective bargaining contracts vary in their length and specificity. Due to rapid growth in collective bargaining at all levels of government, increasing numbers of public sector employees are included under the provisions of bilaterally negotiated labor agreements. A recent study estimated that about 38 percent of the executive branch federal employees and approximately 21 percent of state and local government employees were covered by collective bargaining contracts (Craft, 1972: 30).

Gradually, in many state jurisdictions, attempts are being made to incorporate specific provisions as they relate to contract management. This helps reduce the psychological worries and contractual constraints experienced by the public managers in carrying out their management activities to allocate or utilize human resources. Since administration of collective bargaining agreements covers various phases of contractual relationships between the employer and employee, it is highly desirable for state or local governments to free the will of their managers (administrators) from the fear of union activities by establishing mandatory policies to deal with the problem of employee militancy.

UNFAIR LABOR PRACTICES

Any actions or practices employed by either employers or unions may be characterized as unfair if they are defined by the statute in effect as being unfair labor practices. Such practices are better defined (as an illustration) by the federal Taff-Hartley Act, after which most states have chosen to pattern their legislative measures. As was the case with the scope of bargaining agreements, provisions for unfair labor practices are remarkably similar. Most of them have simply followed the provisions of the Taft-Hartley Act.

Of the 28 states that have stipulated by statute unfair labor practices, the state of New York has a wider scope of provisions, and they are stipulated in the statute for both employer and employees. In all, 16 states have chosen to follow the Taff-Hartley Act provisions with little or no deviation. The remaining nine states have chosen to add to the original act. But the additions merely spell out the details.

Hawaii has also added as unfair practices: violation of agreement, refusal to participate in good faith in impasse procedures, and refusal to comply with statute.

Kansas, in addition to the Taft-Hartley Act, has also included avoiding impasse procedures and the strike or lockout as unfair labor practices.

Maine provides that neither the employer nor employee can be black-listed. *Massachusetts* has included that the strike and violation of the terms of an agreement are unfair labor practices. *Minnesota* not only includes the strike, but violation of orders of the public employment relations board, and refusal to abide by arbitration award. *Nevada's* unfair labor practices include the violation of an agreement and the refusal to comply with statute. *New Mexico* law states that violation of election provisions is an unfair practice.

Oregon is a special case, since this state has stipulated the Taft-Hartley provisions for employers only. For employees, only the strike is an unfair practice. *Pennsylvania* law states that refusal to comply with arbitration awards, violation of agreements, and certain strikes are unfair practices.

In addition to unfair labor practices stipulated in the Taft-Hartley Act, *Vermont* has added discrimination as an unfair practice for employers, and strikes as unfair for employees. *Wisconsin* provisions include violation of agreements and the strike as unfair practices.

The remaining 27 states follow the Taft-Hartley law very closely. The fact that so many states chose to incorporate similar provisions in their laws may be indicative of its suitability to their political environment. Perhaps, the Taft-Hartley Act serves to meet the needs of that particular state or a particular group of public employees. The second possibility is that Taft-Hartley Act provided a good model for unfair labor practice provisions, so it was adopted, with little thought or deliberation over what types of activities should be labeled as unfair. There is no method of telling which description is a more accurate picture of reality.

UNION SECURITY PROVISIONS

Union security is a term which describes laws that serve to protect the employee and the union from encroachment by management, nonunion employees, and/or raids by competing unions.

There are now 30 states that provide some type of union security measures. Throughout the nation, there are different types of union security procedures. The one most commonly referred to is the dues check-off (deduction). In this type of arrangement, the employer deducts from the pay of all employees who are members of the union in the bargaining unit fees and membership dues and turns this money over to the union. The employer is authorized to do this usually by written consent of each individual employee. This written consent of each individual employee. This written consent is also usually terminated at the end of one year or when the bargaining contract expires.

A second common type of union security in public employment is called the union shop. This type of security lets the employer hire whomever he pleases, yet all new employees are then required to join the union within a specified period of time. This type of security also requires the employee to either remain a member or pay union dues for the duration of the present bargaining contract.

A third type of union security, which is also found in public employment, is the agency shop. Under this type of provision all employees are required (in the bargaining unit) to pay dues or assessments to the collective bargaining agent for service expenses incurred in negotiations. Nonunion employees are not required to join the union as a condition of employment.

Of course, some states employ one of these three types of security in a variety of modifications and variations. However, these are the basic types of security provisions now in use in public employment.

Table 6 provides adequate information on the states with union security provisions, as well as the type of provision, and the employee groups which are covered. It is apparent that many states have chosen not to provide union security measures to all employee groups. State workers, in particular, are not often covered by union security provisions in many states. Perhaps one of the reasons for this is the great diversity of employees on state payrolls. Certain types of tasks and employment may suffer from a constraining influence provided by union security procedures.

TABLE 6
Union Security Provisions Provided by State Laws

State	Type of Employee					
	State	Local	Firemen	Police	Teachers	Other
Alaska	U.S.	U.S.	U.S.	N.A.P.	N.A.P.	
Connecticut	- -	D.C.	D.C.	D.C.	- -	
Delaware	D.C.	D.C.	D.C.	D.C.	D.C.	
Dist. of Columbia	- -	M.A.S.	M.A.S.	M.A.S.	- -	
Florida	- -	- -	- -	- -	D.C.	
Hawaii	D.C.	D.C.	D.C.	D.C.	D.C.	
Kansas	- -	D.C.	D.C.	D.C.	- -	
Kentucky	- -	- -	D.C.[a]	- -	- -	
Louisiana	D.C.[b]	D.C.[b]	D.C.[b]	D.C.[b]	D.C.[b]	

TABLE 6 (Continued)

State	Type of Employee					
	State	Local	Firemen	Police	Teachers	Other
Maine	– –	– –	D.C.	D.C.	D.C.	
Maryland	– –	– –	– –	– –	D.C.	
Massachusetts	– –	A.S.	A.S.	A.S.	A.S.	
Michigan	– –	A.S.	A.S.	A.S.	A.S.	
Minnesota	D.C.	D.C.	D.C.	D.C.	D.C.	
Missouri	– –	D.C.	D.C.	– –	– –	
Nebraska	– –	D.C.	D.C.	D.C.	– –	
Nevada	– –	– –	D.C.	D.C.	D.C.	
New Hampshire	D.C.	– –	– –	D.C.	D.C.	
New Jersey	– –	D.C.	D.C.	D.C.	D.C.	
New Mexico	A.S.P.	– –	– –	– –	– –	
New York	D.C.	D.C.	D.C.	D.C.	D.C.	
North Dakota	– –	D.C.	D.C.	D.C.	– –	
Oklahoma	– –	– –	D.C.	D.C.	—	
Oregon	– –	D.C.	D.C.	D.C.	– –	
Pennsylvania	D.C.	D.C.	– –	D.C.	D.C.	
Rhode Island	A.S.[c]	– –	– –	A.S.[c]	– –	
South Dakota	– –	D.C.	– –	D.C.	D.C.	
Vermont	– –	U.S.	U.S.	– –	– –	
Washington	D.C.	D.C.	D.C.	D.C.	– –	D.C. (Univ. teach.)
Wisconsin	– –	F.S.A.[d]	F.S.A.[d]	F.S.A.[d]	F.S.A.[d]	

Sources: U.S. Department of Labor (1973: 2-37) Summary of State Policy Regulations. Washington, D.C.: U.S. Gov't Printing Office.

U.S. — Union Shop
A.S. — Agency Shop
D.C. — Dues Check-off or deduction
N.A.P. — Negotiation Agreements to Provide for Procedures

M.A.S. — Modified Agency Shop
A.S.P. — Agency Shop Prohibited
F.S.A. — Fair Share Agreement

a. Dues deduction required

b. Employing authority may elect whether or not to make deductions

c. Mandatory

d. Subject to employer or employee organization petition for a referendum

V. THE MODEL LEGISLATION: QUEST AND RESPONSE

Significant developments in the past few years emphasize that the managing of labor relations in the public sector is a continuing and urgent problem. Although most states forbid public employees to strike, work stoppages of government personnel at all levels have been skyrocketing. At the same time, the right of government workers to organize is now recognized in more than two-thirds of the states. Regarding labor management policies for state and local government, the Advisory Commission on Inter-Governmental Relations (1969) asserted that:

> State efforts will have little significance unless there is appropriate machinery to resolve recognition and representation disputes, ensure adherence by all parties to the law, and provide the means of facilitating the resolution of controversies arising out of employer-employee impasses [quoted in *New Proposals for 1972*, ACIR, 1971: 71].

In the above assertion, there is inherent a strong desire not only to set up regulatory machinery but to promote enactment of comprehensive legislation emphasizing affirmative action and the acceptance of the idea to "meet and confer in good faith." States are already familiar with this idea and are heading in the direction of establishing necessary laws. Yet, there is much that remains to be achieved in various state and local jurisdictions. In order to provide a framework for the regulation of public employer-employee relations, the ACIR provided two model bills which may be adopted by different states with necessary modifications to fit their local conditions. However, the thinking of public managers (administrators) towards public employer-employee relations and their regulation by comprehensive legislation has been reflected in some concern about the impact of such legislation on program policies and the merit system. Since the proposed model bills take into account the utility of merit systems and management decision-making responsibility, the question of merit system vs. collective bargaining has been examined in this section with a focus on the applicability of proposed model bills toward promoting developmental legislation. It is important to note that a proper understanding or perspective on this issue will pave the way to an orderly conduct of public employer-employee relations in the future.

MERIT SYSTEM v. COLLECTIVE BARGAINING

The merit system has long been in existence in public employment. In a traditional sense, it was first intended to eliminate old tenants of the spoils system and political patronage from the state and local governments. It was also intended to facilitate the entry of qualified individuals into the service of the state. The growth of unionism and collective bargaining among public employees has created fears in the minds of many public administrators related to the effectiveness of the merit system. The argument states that the theory of collective bargaining and its practice in certain areas directly conflicts with the principles of the merit system. There is, however, a continuing debate as to whether there really are conflicts between the two.

The original purpose of the merit system was rather narrowly confined to serve as a protection in the selection of personnel through the use of such institutions as a civil service commission or personnel board at state and local levels. Traditionally, the commission assumed the responsibilities of defining and classifying jobs, preparing and administering competitive examinations, and insuring through proper appeals and administrative procedures that employees were hired and retained, as well as promoted, on the basis of merit rather than on the basis of political ideology or affiliation. From such practices emerged the idea that the civil service should be a corps of career-oriented civil servants who are relatively unattached to management.

The argument forwarded by many unions against the career stagnation in civil service centers around the contention that in many states and municipalities the system has become overextended. In effect, it has become a sort of personnel department for the governing body, and many employees see the system as part of management (Derber, 1969: 17-18).

Employees and unions have further argued that basically the merit system programs are just "no good." Merit is not the prevailing principle even where civil service systems exist. In most cases, personal influences and favoritism prevail. As for these claims, some may be substantiated in certain areas, but not for the nation as a whole.

Many unions and some employees have expressed a desire to have the merit system despite the fact that in some areas it is "still filled with spoils and political favoritism, and the paternalistic attitudes of management." Yet, others maintain that many of these deficiencies in the system could be improved upon and not thrown away (Connery and Farr, 1970: 59-62).

On the other hand, many administrators greatly fear the coming of unionization. They fear that unions want to replace merit principles with negotiated contracts. In their opinion, should unions be successful in achieving their objectives, the civil service commission would be stripped of all of its duties except recruitment; the rest of its former duties would be written into negotiated contracts. There is further fear of agreements that are negotiated in secret. Of course, all public laws are passed through open legislative sessions. Yet, contract negotiations occur behind closed doors, where the age-old merit principles could be bargained away without the "slightest hesitancy." Furthermore, many administrators cannot reconcile merit principles with such union practices as exclusive recognition, agency shops, or union shops. This type of coercion into joining the union (paying the dues), when such practices have little to do with actual job performance, is greatly disturbing to many administrators. Finally, many administrators reason that the institution and growth of public employee collective bargaining will inevitably lead to the end of "equal pay for equal work," a long standing merit principle (Nigro, 1970: 58-59).

Basically, most administrators fear that the process of collective bargaining and an ever-widening scope of negotiation in secret sessions will ultimately eradicate the merit system. At present this fear is unsubstantiated. In areas where public employee negotiations are and have been taking place, flexibility has been the rule of the game. Moreover, a merit system may be protected either through statute itself or by the procedures established by a local employee relations board. Some states have given new responsibilities to civil service commissions that are somewhat similar to those of employee relations boards.

Broadly, it seems that the reasons why employees join unions have little to do with the basic tenets of the merit system. Most union members see the basic purpose of their union as their collective bargaining agent, responsible for negotiating better wages and working conditions for themselves (Christrup, 1969: 119). It seems to have very little relation to the operation and principles of a civil service system. The basic fear about the destruction of the merit system arises when the issues at the bargaining table continue to expand. Perhaps far in the future, the merit system as we know it today may go through an evolutionary change. Undoubtedly, any erosion that may threaten to impinge upon the principles of merit can be lessened by legislative measures and administrative regulations. Scope of bargaining can be more precisely defined depending upon the nature of the issue being negotiated. At the present, the catch-all phrase "working conditions" is so vague and ambiguous that many things may be inferred. Whether there is really a conflict between collective bargaining and the merit system ultimately depends upon some critical factors. That is, what do unions want? What types of changes do they want to effect? How and to what extent will they go to accomplish their objectives? Finally, what are the issues that may and may not be discussed over a bargaining table?

By determining the answers to these questions in any given area and situation, it should be possible to estimate how well the merit principle should be able to survive. However, there seems to be a tacit consensus among most public employees that they do not want to do away with the merit system. Most employees feel that the system itself has provided them with many fringe benefits such as job security, and they further appriciate the "protection" offered them by the merit system.

It must also be remembered that some areas of public employment are not covered by the merit system. In such a situation, many public employees still capitalize on old rules of political patronage. Many will argue that examinations for recruitment on the basis of merit serve to screen out disadvantaged persons. Yet what of the spoils system that still survives? In many areas, these systems serve to screen out not only disadvantaged people and minorities, but other groups not favorably disposed to the administration in that jurisdiction.

It may be true that in many areas the merit system has definite shortcomings and deficiencies. But is this any worse than having no system at all? Many public employees would welcome the institution of merit system because it offers a certain degree of fairness and privilege to all public employees without any distinction or discrimination.

Undoubtedly, the merit system will be with us in the future. In some cases, it may be modified due to the influences of collective bargaining, and in some cases it may even be strengthened. The supposed conflicts between the two seem to arise not out of any inherent conflict or any inherent characteristics that may set them in opposition to each other, but out of psychological constraints experienced by the public managers due to lack of professional skills and proper understanding of the craft of managing.

Apparent conflict between the two is developed between the two extremes of human behavior that advocate one over the other. There is, in a sense, very little effort to identify the characteristics and problems of each, in an attempt to combine the two into a smooth overall process. What is apparently happening is that the two groups who cling to one system over the other assume that the system they oppose is diametrically opposed to their own. Thus, the conflict that arises is not necessarily inherent in merit principles. It is the operational dynamics and prevailing environment that determine the degree of disagreement and thus becomes a product of behavior and interaction among groups of human beings who support or disdain them.

The merit system is not in inherent conflict with the institution of collective bargaining. However, the operation of the merit system is substantially affected by the collective bargaining process. The operation of one does not have to hinder, impede, or destroy the operation of the other. Both can be made to coexist with little or no friction between them. The success or failure of coexistence will depend greatly on the types of laws and regulations that are created, and subsequently the way these laws are implemented. Jurisdictional authorities must be redefined in some cases. In most instances, the scope of bargaining must be more closely defined in order to insure the continuation of each system or institution. With the right legislation, and the right procedures of implementation, there is no reason why the two should be in opposition, or even in competition.

As has been stated earlier, many jurisdictions do not have required legislation concerning the regulation of public labor-management relations. Thus, in the interest of stable labor-management relations, it is imperative that necessary legislation be enacted by those states. From the viewpoint of developing a proper perspective on public labor-management relations, an analytical discussion of model bills will be profitable to all those jurisdictions that do not have formal policy regulations.

MODEL LAWS FOR PUBLIC EMPLOYEE RELATIONS

Adoption of any employee relations law must logically be concerned with the feasibility of implementing such a measure. Obviously, if a particular state has never experienced any trouble with public employees, there is going to be a great deal of difficulty in designing measures and establishing procedures that will operate efficiently and smoothly. Of course, lessons and experiences of other states in this area should be helpful. The first logical step in the adoption of state labor legislation is to identify the need for such legislation. At this point, it seems obvious that such laws are needed in every state. Without legislation on the books, states are needlessly tying the hands of their bureaucrats and municipal officials. The states in the South are especially in need of legislation in this area.[6] The South may wish to bury its head in the sand, but this will not stop the wave of the future. The need for some type of legislation is now growing critical. When unionism and employee militancy come to a head in the South, the inexperience of officials in dealing with unions and union activity will pose very serious problems for the continuous flow of goods and services to the public. In effect, the nature of public service and the demands for public services, combined with the demands of public employees and growing unions, mean that public officials in states with no procedures and statutes to help control public employee union relations are playing against a very heavily stacked deck. Many local and municipal officials, especially in the South, may not even yet realize the gravity of the entire situation. Probably, in many states, public officials will be rudely awakened to what they do not know, and to what extent many state legislators and executives choose to ignore the problem. When the inevitable happens at the municipal or county level, the small-time mayor and the inexperienced administrator will be left to fend for themselves.

Once the need for legislation has been realized—and enough support has arisen for its passage into law—the right type of law must be designed. The type of law that is needed will depend largely on experience with labor relations and proper enforcement of labor procedures. Obviously, in a state where most administrators have never had to work with employee organizations, the type of law designed should not be one that creates highly sophisticated and complex procedures. In other words, it is not desirable to go from "nothing to everything" at one time. Second, proposed legislation should be somewhat related to the amount and degree of public employee unionization in the state. And measures for the amendment of the law should be easily available to meet the needs of both public employees and administrators.

In effect, while it may be desirable to design an overall plan to approach the implementation or proper procedures and appropriate legislation, based upon the experiences in other states, it should be feasible to approach public employee relations through a number of phases. The first phase would probably consist of the passage of laws. Within this frame of reference, measures must be taken to "reeducate" administrators and to acquaint them with public employee relations. In a given political environment the feasibility and scope of needed law should be very carefully examined. Experiences of other states and model legislation proposed by research institutions or specialized agencies would be extremely helpful in providing various options. It is desirable at this point to examine some model employee legislation.

The Advisory Commission on Intergovernmental Relations (ACIR, New Proposals, 1972: 71-86) has developed model legislation in an attempt to assist in dealing with public employer-employee relations. The commission has developed two types of laws:

(1) a "meet and confer in good faith" law, and
(2) a "collective negotiations" law.[7]

From the viewpoint of developmental legislation in a relatively "inexperienced" state, the meet and confer approach would probably be better. The ACIR prefaces the act by saying it is an act to establish an orderly framework for dealings between employee organizations and employers. The law further states that a "public employee relations agency" is hereby created (hereafter referred to as the agency). This agency is composed of five members appointed by the governor for staggered terms. The agency itself is responsible for appointing mediators, members of fact-finding panels, and so forth, and for fixing the compensation and duties of these persons.

The basic purpose of the agency is to act as a clearinghouse of information relating to conditions of employment for public employees in the state. It should also provide training and technical assistance to public employers, and request from any other public agency such services and information that will lead to better performance. Finally, the agency should establish procedures for preventing unhealthy employment practices. Powers and jurisdiction of the agency are exclusive and nondelegatable.

Section four of the act concerns public employee rights. Public employees shall have the right to form, join, and participate in employee organizations of their own choice. The organizations are designed for the purpose of meeting and conferring with public employers or their representatives for discussing grievances, wages, hours, and other terms and conditions of employment. Employees should also have the right to refuse to join such organizations.

Supervisory employees may be able to form and join their own organizations that do not include nonsupervisory employees. Section six deals with the rights of the public employer. The basic rights granted to the employer are:

(1) to direct the work of his employees;
(2) to hire, promote, assign, transfer, and retain employees in positions within the public agency;

(3) to demote, suspend, or discharge employees for proper cause;

(4) to maintain the efficiency of governmental operations;

(5) to relieve employees from duties because of lack of work or other legitimate reasons;

(6) to take actions necessary for the good of the agency in time of emergency; and

(7) to determine the methods, means, and personnel by which operations may be continued.

Section seven of the act states that public employers must recognize the employee organization and certify the organization as representing a majority of employees in the appropriate unit. At this time, the employer may meet and confer in good faith with the employee organization concerning terms and conditions of employment and the administration of grievances, and enter into a contractual agreement with the employee organization. Should a question of representation arise over the determination of the appropriate unit, the public employee relations agency shall decide the question.

Section eight of the act deals with the rights that accompany formal recognition. The type of recognition offered by the employer will be exclusive and subject to review every 12 months. The public employer further will extend to employees the right of dues deduction upon the submission of written authorization cards by employees. Further, those representatives of the organization will be given time off from their jobs without loss of compensation during normal work hours to meet and confer with the employer.

Section 10 defines the scope of a memorandum agreement. Its scope may extend to all areas related to employment conditions and employer-employee relations, including but not necessarily limited to wages, hours, and other conditions of employment. The scope of the memorandum may not include proposals relating to any subject preempted by federal or state law or municipal charter; public employee rights in this act; public employer rights; or the authority and power of any civil service commission, personnel board, agency, or of its agents established by constitution, statute, charter, or special act, to set and create standards of recruitment, conduct, grade merit examinations, and to rate candidates in the order of their relative excellence from which appointments or promotions may be made. A memorandum of agreement may contain a grievance procedure culminating in advisory arbitration of unresolved grievances.

A memorandum is implemented in the following manner. Once agreement has been reached between the employee organization and the employer, they shall jointly prepare a memorandum and, within two weeks, present it to the governing body (legislative body or agent with legislative powers) for determination. The governing body, after receiving a report from the chief financial officer of the public agency as to the probable effect of the memorandum agreement upon the agency, will take appropriate action. Should a settlement be reached, the governing body will be responsible for implementing the settlement in the form of a law, ordinance, rule, regulation, and so forth. If the governing body rejects the memorandum, the matter is returned to the two parties for further deliberation.

Section 12 deals with the resolution of disputes that may arise in the course of discussions. Either the employer or the agency may define a situation where an impasse exists. At this point, the agency will help resolve the impasse through the use of mediation at agency expense. Failure to resolve the dispute will mean the initiation of fact-finding procedures that will culminate in recommendations delivered to both parties. Should this fail to resolve the dilemma, these findings of the fact-finding panel will be made public. If the impasse has still not been resolved, both the employer and employee organization must present their respective cases before the governing body, which shall take whatever action it deems necessary in the public interest.

Section 13 defines certain practices by either employee organizations or employer as prohibited and as "evidence of bad faith." The employer may not:

(1) interfere with rights of public employees as granted in the act;

(2) intervene in the formation or operation of the employee organization;

(3) encourage or discourage membership in the organization through discrimination in hiring or promotion;

(4) discharge or discriminate against an employee who has carried out proper procedures regarding the filing of grievance procedures, given testimony, or for joining, forming, or assisting in the employee organization;

(5) refuse to meet and confer;

(6) deny the rights accompanying certification of formal recognition;

(7) blacklist any employee or organization because of their organizational activities; and

(8) avoid mediation and fact-finding endeavors, in the event of impasse.

Public employees or employee organizations are prohibited from:

(1) interfering with the rights of employees under this act;

(2) interfering with the rights of employers under this act;

(3) refusing to meet and confer;

(4) avoiding mediation and fact-finding efforts; and

(5) engaging in a strike.

As to the violations of prohibited practices, Section 14 states that charges and evidence of violation should be given to the agency. The accused party is notified by the agency and is given one week to answer charges. A hearing is then held by the agency, at which time evidence will be taken, both parties may be represented by counsel, and witnesses will be summoned. The agency shall determine as to findings of fact and either dismiss the complaint or determine that a violation has been committed. Should the accused party be found to be committing a violation, the agency shall petition an appropriate court to punish the accused. The agency's record of hearings shall also be submitted to the court. Persons aggrieved by the findings of the agency may have those findings reviewed by the court of appropriate jurisdiction. Otherwise all decisions of the public employee relations agency will be final.

Section 16 of the act requires that all employee organizations must register with the agency, and submit annual reports to the agency covering the officers and agents of the organization; they must provide standards and safeguards over the conduct of organizational elections, for the regulation of trusteeship and judicial responsibilities of organizational officers, and for the maintenance of accounting and fiscal control of the organization, as well as regular financial reports. Failure to comply with any of these obligations will mean that the organization will not be recognized for the purposes of meet and confer discussions.

This model act may serve as the first step in the development of any states' comprehensive public employee relations laws. As such it represents the first step in the effort to meet what every state in this nation must face in the future. It serves, in effect, as developmental legislation that may help develop and build institutions and procedures for the smooth administration of employee relations, at any level within the state. The ACIR has also developed a "collective negotiations" model law that centers mainly around bilateral negotiations.[8] There does not seem to be a great difference between the two model bills proposed by the ACIR except that the collective negotiations alternative places major emphasis on bilateralism in labor-management relations. It establishes a public employee relations agency that would enjoy greater scope of its powers in matters of determining bargaining units and their exclusive certification, in hearing unfair labor charges, and in instituting court action to stop them.

VI. LESSONS OF THE PAST AND FUTURE CHALLENGES

In preceding sections of this paper, an attempt was made to analyze the types of measures that many states across the nation have taken to deal with public labor-management relations. Many of the statutes and administrative measures have been brought into existence by a growing awareness and a strong desire among public employees to directly participate in those decisions that affect their working lives. At this time, it would surely be unfounded to reason that such desires and needs would suddenly disappear.

Laws were also necessitated due to the fact that public employees have utilized the instrument of employee unions to make their demands known and their grievances heard. The phenomenal growth of public employee unions just in the past 10 years would logically indicate that no area of the country will be able to escape the impact of such growth. It would also be naive to try to wish unions away, or pretend that they do not exist. The trend indicates that the growth and strength of unions will continue to accelerate in the future. Only those public administrators who know the craft of managing public labor-management relations process will be comfortable or successful.

Complicating this picture is the ever-rising demand for public service which places the administrator in a very unenviable position. On the one hand, he must cope with his subordinates who demand more for their services. On the other hand, he must meet the demands of the public at large, whose whetted appetites are fueling the insatiable desires for public services, and not the costs of those services. Considering these factors in assessing the job of the administrator, the demands and constraints of his job should not be forgotten. In trying to satisfy both of these demands placed upon him, the administrator must also be concerned with the limitations on his own ability to act. He must be aware of the fiscal resources that are available for any type of concerted action. He must also be aware of legal limitations on his ability to take action, since he is an agent of the public. He must always be conscious of the political environment in which he operates, which may serve to severely limit his sphere of action. To sum all of this up, perhaps the greatest liability or asset the administrator may have is his ability or inability to cope with the complexities of his work and environment. He cannot be a type of bureaucratic politician and attempt to play off one side against the other (public demands over public employee demands, or vice versa), because he owes an obligation to both. Moreover, he is caught in a situation that would appear as if both sides are playing against the middle—and he is in the middle. He must try to satisfy all of the demands that are placed upon him, no matter at what level of government (federal, state, or local) he is placed.

From this description, it can be readily seen that the public administrator will be the focal point of a number of serious and divisive pressures from his immediate environment. Given this fact, it is imperative that statutes that give him some kind of framework, and that guidelines to deal with the onslaught of public unionism be enacted in states that presently have no such legislation. As it now stands, these states are so inadequately prepared to deal with this problem that the administrator is left to fend for himself without any legal support. Left to continually operate in such a manner not only will the administrator suffer, but so will employees under him, not to mention the public which they serve. In the final analysis, as is so often the story, the general public will have to pay the price of work stoppages and chaotic conditions that are partly the result of legislative inaction. It is now time to "get out the story" that the reality of the not too distant future is upon us. The period of waiting to see what happens and ignoring the facts before us is over. We can no longer demand or expect that public employees may be subjected to the paternalistic, arbitrary actions of public managers, as they have been in the past.

It has also been the prevailing attitude of much of the general public that unions only mean trouble and expense. While this attitude seems now to be slowly dying out in many areas, it is apparent that it is still largely dominant in Southern region and in a few rural states. This negative attitude may bring more public suffering, if the civic communities are hard hit by public employee strikes. It is this negative attitude which prompts some southern state legislators to oppose passage of any legislative measure.[9] This type of attitude itself may, through a number of channels, lead to a volatile atmosphere that involves the strike and the threat of strike, leading to economic chaos and general frustration. Moreover, it is precisely this type of attitude that is misleading. The public should be informed of the alternatives now at hand. When the facts are brought to light, there is no choice: laws, procedures, and processes must be developed to adequately solve the problem. Furthermore, the continued presence of such obstacles prevents the furthering of the goals of government. The process of negotiations concerning terms and conditions of employment between employers and employees is an effective method of meeting governmental goals. Many workers in the public service have developed an intense feeling of alienation because of the practices of the past. As more employees are inducted into the public sector, this feeling will continue to grow. A responsible employee organization can develop a voice that can serve to eliminate this alienation and to provide better relations for all of those concerned. Moreover, negotiations will serve as an effective communications system that will be utilized to effectively bind both sides of the bargaining table together as well as provide both parties with the information and motivation necessary to render better service to the public. The institutionalization of bargaining processes will also help the administrator to learn new supervisory techniques in order to cope with organizational and administrative problems that develop with the acquisition of new technology. From this point of view, the development of unionism and the resultant establishment of procedures for negotiations between employer and employee will be desirable not only for public employees, but for public management, and ultimately, for the public at large. The question at this point then, is not whether to institute public employee relations laws, but how and to what degree should they be effective and comprehensive.

It is perhaps inevitable though, that many cities, counties, and states will be caught unprepared, and will have to learn the hard way after the damage has already occurred. There have already been attempts in the Congress to enact omnibus public employee relations laws that would force all states to develop regulatory policies and procedures. Although these measures did not pass, this is an important indication of what soon will happen.[10]

Assuming the current trends in the growth of unionism remain constant, which is a conservative estimate, states will have no choice but to develop the right types of laws. Necessary legislation must be enacted not only with an eye to future needs, but with an eye to past experiences. Measures should provide for a number of considerations such as the protection of merit principles, public interest, and management rights. The laws should also incorporate that the duties and responsibilities of presently constituted civil service systems cannot be bargained away. Furthermore, adequate provision for the protection of employee rights should also be considered. This must include measures that would keep employers from interfering in the formation and/or operation of any legally constituted employee organization. Also included should be measures that would prevent any discrimination by the employers against those employees who play active roles in the organization.

Public employee relations laws must also make provisions for the protection of employer's rights. These must prohibit employee organizations from interfering in the effective and orderly operation of the public agency, or in the formulation of program policies, or even in the employers' prerogatives to "manage" the organization. Union security provisions and unfair labor practices should also be contained in any type of developmental legislation.

The proper protection for the maintenance and efficient delivery of services to the general public should be the basic goal of the public manager. It is the public interest that the government intends to serve. If this not be the case, perhaps it would be more advantageous to speak in terms of what is good for government. Privileges of the sovereign become more meaningful if they serve some public purpose and promote the long cherished values of the society.

In sum, on the basis of this analysis of laws and procedures in various states, the following inferences could be drawn:

(1) States that have no laws and procedures are ill prepared to deal with the problems of labor-management relations.

(2) The passage of necessary laws is negatively affected by dogmatic views and legalistic considerations.

(3) Lack of adequate laws to deal with the problem would involve much greater risk and cost for all parties concerned.

(4) Positive action is needed to establish policies through developmental legislation.

(5) Decentralized legislative and administrative measures will help cope with state and local diversities.

(6) State sovereignty, management rights, and public interest should be understood in the light of current social change and impact of judicial policy on public labor-management relations.

(7) If the states fail to devise effective policy measures through legislation, the federal government may step in to fill the gap by passing an omnibus type legislation.

If the public does not demand such action, the party that will undoubtedly incur greater loss and face inconvenience and frustration will inevitable be the public itself. Above all, the basic issue to be settled in the future remains how a thriving and unavoidable unionization of public work force could be harnessed to serve public interest, equity, excellence, and stable public labor-management relations.

NOTES

1. In a recent case (390 AFL-CIO v. County of Alameda, 62 LC 52, 245: Calif., 1970, Ct. App.) on the question of "amnesty" for striking public employees, the court of appeals remanded the county officials for not ignoring such provisions entered into during collective bargaining sessions. In this case, the "modern view" of public labor relations—that is, stable labor relations—took precedence over the traditional view of government sovereignty which treats such strikes as akin to treason and, as such, deserving of strict punishment. Further affirmation of this changing concept of sovereignty is illustrated in Wheatley v. City of Covington, 68 LC 52, 781: KY, 1972, Civ. Ct. Here the court forced the city to pay raises to its employees as per a collective bargaining agreement despite the fact that budgetary approval was lacking from the council. Further, state debt regulations forbidding the assumption of increased obligation were held not applicable to the situation. In the case of Ball v. City of Coachella, 55 LC 51, 730: Calif., 1967, the court upheld that public officials, who strike at the will of elected officials, may not be fired for taking part in union activities.

2. In southern states, most of the strikes by local government employees during 1968-1970 represented mixed blessings, but they were mainly directed toward union recognition. With a few exceptions, most of them were successful and also demonstrated that these states were not adequately prepared, due to lack of required legislation, to deal with matters related to public labor-management relations. The recent strike by 300 nonuniformed employees in the city of Little Rock further demonstrates a need for collective bargaining law in the state. Despite a strict warning from the city manager, Mr. McMullin, about the illegality of strike, the workers did not return to their jobs (Arkansas Gazette, August 15, 1974: 3A).

3. In an attempt to develop an analytical framework for a comparative analysis of state laws and procedures dealing with public labor-management relations, it was realized that because of diversity in laws, procedures, and employee groups covered it will be unmanageable for a short study like this to develop such a framework which could apply to all states and truly represent their level of administrative, economic, and political development. It was not possible to comprehend all environmental variables or inputs and develop a valid or acceptable frame of reference. In order to develop a comparative perspective on public labor-management relations policy, it was realized that the type of collective bargaining rights enjoyed by the public and private sector employees comparatively will provide a reasonably acceptable analytical framework to classify different states as "progressive," "intermediate," and "primitive." These categories, in any way, do not represent an overall status of politico-administrative development in different states.

4. Some of the important aspects covered in this section include: provisions dealing with the creation of regulatory agency, determination of collective bargaining unit, resolution of impasse procedures, methods of negotiation, and the nature of centralized v. decentralized administrative control.

5. However, the firefighters in Idaho are not supposed to go on strike during the term of a written agreement (Idaho Laws of 1970, chap. 138).

6. J. William Becker, president of Arkansas State AFL-CIO, pointed out on August 14, 1974, that the strike by 300 nonuniformed city employees at Little Rock clearly "demonstrates the need for collective bargaining law in Arkansas." He further stated that "had there been collective bargaining law, there probably would not have been a strike" (Arkansas Gazette, August 15, 1974: 3A). With much uncertainty, the current legal parameters are determined by the Constitutional Amendment No. 34 (1944) and title 81, Section 201 of the Arkansas Statutes which was invoked in the case of *Self v. Taylor* (217 Ark. 953). A further affirmation of the right of municipal employees to join unions came in *Potts v. Hay* (229 Ark. 1958, 830) and *City of Fort Smith v. Arkansas State Council No. 38, AFSCME, AFL-CIO, et al.,* (433 S.W. 2d, 1968, 153).

7. The full text of the ACIR model bills is provided in New Proposals for 1972: ACIR Legislative Program (ACIR, 1971: 71-98)

8. The ACIR favors the meet and confers approach, but it has proposed two alternative model bills—one incorporating meet and confer approach and the other concentrating on a negotiations approach. Actually, the differences between the two model bills are not great. In general, the collective negotiations alternative places greater stress on bilateralism in employer-employee relations. The meet and confer bill makes clear the right of public employees to join or not to join employee organizations.

9. For instance, legislative measure were introduced three times (1969, 1971, and 1973) in Arkansas providing collective bargaining rights to state and municipal employees. They failed to pass as most of the conservative legislators and administrators in the state vigorously opposed the passage of any such law. In 1973, two separate but identical bills (S.B. 183 & H.B. 266) were introduced simultaneously in the state senate and house extending collective bargaining rights to public employees. The bill No. 183 was passed by the senate but the similar measure died in a house committee without reaching a vote in the house. It is expected to be a major issue of 1975 legislative session. Still, a negative attitude among legislators and some administrators continues to be a major hurdle in the passage of such law.

10. ACIR has realized the fact that the states must act before the national Congress approves proposed bills to mandate uniform public employee relations policies for all state and local governments. AFSCME, NEA, and the Unions for National Legislation for Public Unions have been sponsoring such bills for several years (H.R. 7684, H.R. 9324, H.R. 8677). Representative Frank Thompson (N.J.) also introduced a bill (H.R. 12532) in the Congress and his special subcommittee held hearings in 1972. This bill seeks to bring all state and local employees under the National Labor Relations Act. Although there is a general opposition to "federal mandating," Jerry Wurf, president of AFSCME, believes that if states will not act, the federal government should do so in the nation's interest. Obviously, he is not alone who holds such views; the NEA bill also reflects the same concern (Nigro, 1973: 316-317 and U.S. Cong., House Spl. Subcommittee on Labor, Hearings, 1972: 1-59).

REFERENCES

Advisory Commission on Inter-Governmental Relations (1971) New Proposals for 1972: ACIR Legislative Program. Washington, D.C.

ANDERSON, H. J. [ed.] (1968) Public Employee Organization and Bargaining. Washington, D.C.: Bureau of National Affairs.

BAKKE, E. (1970) "Reflections on the future of public sector bargaining" Monthly Labor Rev. 93 (July): 21-25.

BERGER, H. F. (1970) "The old order giveth way to the new: a comparison of Executive Order 10988 with Executive Order 11491." Labor Law J. 21 (February): 79-87.

Bureau of National Affairs (1968) Public Employee Organization and Bargaining. Washington, D.C.: Bur. of Natl. Affairs.

CHRISTRUP, H. J. (1969) "Why do government employees join unions?" in R. Woodworth and R. B. Peterson (eds.) Collective Negotiation for Public and Professional employers. Glenview, Ill.: Scott, Foresman.

COHANY, H. P. and L. M. DEWEY (1970) "Union membership among government employees." Monthly Labor Rev. 93 (July): 15-20.

CONNERY, R. H. and W. V. FARR [eds.] (1970) Unionization of Municipal Employees. Proceedings of the Acad. of Pol. Sci. 30.

CRAFT, J. (1972) "Notes on the administration of collective bargaining agreements." Personnel Admin. & Public Personnel Rev. I (July-August): 30-33.

——— (1972) "Notes on the administration of collective bargaining agreements." Personnel Admin. and Public Personnel Rev. 1 (July-August): 30-33.

CROUCH, W. (1968) Employer-Employee Relations in Council-Manager Cities. Washington, D.C.: Internatl. City Management Assn.

DERBER, M. (1969) "Who negotiates for the public employees? in Keith Ocheltree (ed.) Perspective in Public Employee Negotiation. Chicago: Public Personnel Assn.

DOWLING, E. T. (1974) Municipal Collective Bargaining: The Connecticut Experience under MERA. Storrs: Inst. of Public Service.

——— [ed.] (1972) Municipal Collective Bargaining: The Connecticut Experience under MERA. Storrs: Inst. of Public Service.

FALLON, W. J. (1970) "For some order in public employee Bargaining." Labor Law J. 21 (July): 434-437.

GAWTHORP, L. C. (1971) Administrative Politics and Social Change. New York: St. Martin Press.

GERHART, P. F. (1974) Political Activity by Public Employee Organizations at the Local Level: Threat or Promise? Chicago: Internatl. Personnel Management Assn.

GOLDBERG, J. P. (1972) "Public employee developments in 1971." Monthly Labor Rev. 95 (January): 56-66.

——— (1970) "Changing policies in public employee labor relations." Monthly Labor Rev. 93 (July): 5-14.

HAMPTON, R. E. (1974) "Unions and the public employee." Civil Service J. 14 (January-March): 5-9.

HELBURN, I. B. (1971) Public Employer-Employee Relations in Texas: Contemporary and Emerging Developments. Austin: Inst. of Public Affairs.

HEPPLE, B. A. and P. O'HIGGINS (1971) Public Employee Trade Unionism in the United Kingdom. Ann Arbor: Inst. of Labor Industrial Relations.

HILL, G. E. (1970) "Collective bargaining for state employees." Connecticut Government 24 (Winter): 1-5.

HORTON, R. D. (1973) Municipal Labor Relations in New York City. New York: Praeger.

KAYE, S. and A. MARSH (1973) International Manual on Collective Bargaining for Public Employees. New York: Praeger.

KOCHAN, T. (1973) Resolving Internal Management Conflicts for Labor Negotiations. Chicago: Internatl. Personnel Management Assn.

KRAJCIK, R. S. (1974) "Labor-management relations in state and local government: nature, extent, and impact of judicial involvement." Kent, Ohio: Kent State University (unpubl. Ph.D. dissertation).

KRINSKY, E. B. (1970) "Avoiding public strikes—lessons from recent strike activity." Labor Law J. 21 (August): 464-471.

LIVINSEN, H. M. (1971) Collective Bargaining by British Local Authority Employees. Ann Arbor: Inst. of Labor and Industrial Relations.

MACY, J. W. (1972) "The role of bargaining in the public," pp. 5-19 in S. Zagoria (ed.) Public Workers and Public Unions. Englewood Cliffs, N.J.: Prentice-Hall.

McKELVEY, C.S.J., et al. (1970) New Horizons in Public Employee Bargaining. Chicago: Public Personnel Assn.

MOSKOW, M., J. LOEWENBERG, and E. KOZIARA (1970) Collective Bargaining in Public Employment. New York: Random House.

National Governors' Conference, Executive Committee (1967) Report of the Task Force on State and Local Labor Relations. Chicago: Public Personnel Assn.

––– (1968) Report of the Task Force on State and Local Government Labor Relations. Chicago: Public Personnel Assn.

National League of Cities (1973) National Municipal Policy. Washington: Natl. League of Cities.

NIGRO, F. (1970) "Collective bargaining and the merit system," pp. 55-67 in Connery and Farr (eds.) Proceedings of the Acad. of Pol. Sci. 30.

––– and L. G. NIGRO (1973) Modern Public Administration. New York: Harper & Row.

OCHELTREE, K. [ed.] (1969) Perspective in Public Employee Negotiation. Chicago: Public Personnel Assn.

O'CONNELL, D. W. (1972) Public Sector Labor Relations in Maryland: Issues and Prospects. College Park: Public Sector Labor Relations Conference Board.

O'NEILL, H. (1970) "The growth of municipal employee unions" in Connery and Farr [eds.] (1970) The Academy of Political Science: Proceedings 30 (May-June): 1-13.

Public Management (1973) "Labor-management relations." Special issue 55 (July).

ROBERTS, H. S. (1970) Labor Management Relations in the Public Service. Honolulu: Univ. of Hawaii Press.

SPERO, S. and J. CAPOZZOLA (1973) The Urban Community and its Unionized Bureaucracies. New York: Dunnellen

STENBERG, C. W. (1972) "Labor management relations in state and local government: progress and prospects." Public Admin. Rev. XXXII (March-April): 102-107.

STEPP, J. R. (1974) "The determinants of southern public employee recognition." Public Personnel Management 3 (Jan./Feb.): 59-69.

STIEBER, J. (1973) Public Employee Unionism. Washington, D.C.: Brookings Institution.

––– (1974) "Labor: uncivil servants." Time (July): 41.

U.S. Civil Service Commission (1972) Employee Benefits and Services. Washington: U.S. Gov. Print. Office.

––– (1972) Improving Employment Performance. Washington: U.S. Gov. Print. Office.

––– (1972) Labor-Management Relations in the Public Service. Washington: U.S. Gov. Print. Office.

––– (1972) Personnel Policies and Practices. Washington: U.S. Gov. Print. Office.

––– (1972) State, County, and Municipal Personnel Publications, Washington: U.S. Gov. Print. Office.

––– (1971) Equal Opportunity in Employment Washington: U.S. Gov. Print. Office.

––– (1971) Manpower Planning and Utilization. Washington: U.S. Gov. Print. Office.

––– (1971) Planning Organizing and Evaluating Training Programs. Washington: U.S. Gov. Print. Office.

––– (1971) The Federal Service: History, Organization, and Activities. Washington: U.S. Gov. Print. Office.

––– (1971) The Personnel Management Function: Organization, Staffing and Evaluation. Washington: U.S. Gov. Print. Office.

––– (1970) Employee-Management Relations in the Public Service. Washington: U.S. Gov. Print. Office.

––– (1970) Managing Behavior. Washington: U.S. Gov. Print. Office.

––– (1970) Managing Overseas Personnel. Washington: U.S. Gov. Print. Office.

––– (1970) Personnel Policies and Practices. Washington: U.S. Gov. Print. Office.

––– (1970) Position Classification and Pay in the Federal Government. Washington: U.S. Gov. Print. Office.

––– (1970) Scientists and Engineers in the Federal Government. Washington: U.S. Gov. Print. Office.

––– (1968) Union Recognition in the Federal Government. Washington: U.S. Gov. Print. Office.

U.S. Congress, House of Representatives, Committee on Education and Labor, Special Sub-Committee on Labor (1972) Labor-Management Relations in the Public Sector. Washington: U.S. Gov. Print. Office.

U.S. Department of Labor, Bureau of Labor Statistics (1972) Handbook of Labor Statistics. Washington: U.S. Gov. Print. Office.

––– (1970) "Government work stoppages, 1960, 1969 and 1970," in Stieber, J. (1973) Public Employee Unionism. Washington, D.C.: Brookings Inst.

––– (1970). Work Stoppages in Government 1958-1968. Report 348. Washington: U.S. Gov. Print. Office.

U.S. Department of Labor (1973) Public Employment Program: Annual Report to Congress. Washington: U.S. Gov. Print. Office.

U.S. Department of Labor, Labor Management Services Administration (1973) Summary of State Policy Regulations for Public Sector Labor Relations. Washington: U.S. Gov. Print. Office.

Washington State Personnel Board (1965) Merit System Rules (as amended). Cited in U.S. Dept. of Labor, Labor Management Services Admin. (1973) Summary of State Policy Regulations for Public Section Labor Relations. Washington, D.C.: U.S. Gov. Print. Office.

WILLIAMS, W. J. (1972) "The public service collective bargaining process: toward a new technique." Personnel Admin. & Public Personnel Rev. 1 (July-August): 34-37.

WOODWORTH, R. T. and R. B. PETERSON (1969) Collective Negotiation for Public and Professional Employers. Glenview, Ill.: Scott, Foresman.

WURF, J. (1972) "Labor management relations in public sector," in Report to House Special Committee on Labor (1972). Washington, D.C.: U.S. Gov. Print. Office.

ZACK, A. M. (1970) "Improving mediation and fact-finding in the public sector." Labor Law J. 21 (May): 259-273.

ZAGORIA, S. (1972) "Administration of labor-management relations in local government." Paper delivered in the ASPA Meeting (March): 1-13.

––– [ed.] (1972) Public Workers and Public Unions. Englewood Cliffs, N.J.: Prentice-Hall.

ZEIDLER, F. P. (1972) "An overview of labor management relations in the public service." Public Personnel Rev. 33 (January): 2-5.

APPENDIX

Selected State Laws, Attorney General's Opinions and Court Decisions Pertaining to Public Employee Relations

ALABAMA

Attorney General's Opinion, 1975.
Law of 1967, title 37, chapter 8, article 7, section 450 (3).
Public Acts of 1953, Act 720.

ALASKA

Laws of 1970, chapter 18.
Laws of 1972, chapter 113.

ARKANSAS

City of Fort Smith v. Ark. State Council No. 38 (AFSCME) 433 S.W. 2nd 153 (1968).
Attorney General's Opinion, September 19, 1972.

CALIFORNIA

California Labor Code, sections 1960-1963.
Education Code of 1970, sections 3080-3089.
Laws of 1951, chapter 723.
Laws of 1961, chapter 1964.
Laws of 1971, chapter 254.
Ball v. City of Coachella 55 LC 51,730, Calif. 1967.
San Diego vs. AFSCME Local 127, 87 Cal. Reporter, 258.
390 AFL-CIO v. County of Alameda, 6266 52, 245, Calif. 1970, Ct. App.

CONNECTICUT

Connecticut General Statutes, Public Act 159.
Laws of 1965, Public Act 298.
Senate Bill 406, Laws of 1969.
Norwalk Teachers Assoc. vs. Norwalk Board of Education, 83A, 2d, 482.

DELAWARE

Delaware Code, chapter 13, title 19, sections 1301-1313.
Laws of 1969, chapter 40, title 14.

DISTRICT OF COLUMBIA

Executive Order 70-229, June 19, 1970.

FLORIDA

Dade Co. Classroom Teachers Assoc. vs. Ryan, 225 So. 2d 903, 1969.
Florida Statutes Annotated, chapter 839, 1959.

GEORGIA

Code of Georgia, chapters 89-13, sections 89, 1301; 89, 1304.
House Bill 569, Laws of 1971.

HAWAII

Laws of 1970, Act 191.

IDAHO

Laws of 1970, chapter 138.
House Bill 209, Laws of 1971.

ILLINOIS

Board of Education of Community Unit School Dist. vs. Doris Redding, 207 N.E. 2d 427.

INDIANA

Anderson Federation of Teachers vs. School, City of Anderson, 254 N.E. 2d 329.

IOWA

State Board of Regents vs. Packing Workers, 175 N.W. 2d 110, 1970.

KANSAS

House Bill 1647, Laws of 1970.
Senate Bill 333, Laws of 1971.
Senate Bill 509, Laws of 1972.

KENTUCKY

House Bill 151, Laws of 1972.
House Bill 217, Laws of 1972.
Jefferson Co. Teachers Assoc. vs. Board of Education, 75 LRRM 2486.
Wheatley v. City of Covington, 68 LC 52, 781, KY 1972, Cir. Ct.

LOUISIANA

Laws of 1964, Act 127, sections 890A and 890E.

MAINE

Laws of Maine, chapter 9-A, 1969.

MARYLAND

Laws of 1969, chapter 405, section 160.

MASSACHUSETTS

Laws of 1965, chapter 149.

MICHIGAN

Holland School District vs. Holland Education Assoc. 157 N.W. 2d 206.

MINNESOTA

Senate Bill No. 4, Laws of 1971

MISSOURI

House Bill 166, Laws of 1967.

MONTANA

House Bill 455, Laws of 1971.
Laws of 1969, chapter 320.

NEBRASKA

House Bill 485, Laws of 1967.
Laws of 1974, chapter 178.

NEW JERSEY

Board of Education vs. New Jersey Education Assoc. 69 LRRM 2870.
Laws of 1968, chapter 303.
New Jersey Employer–Employee Relations Act.

NEW HAMPSHIRE

New Hampshire State Code, Laws of 1969, chapter 98C.

NEW MEXICO

New Mexico State Personnel Board Regulations.

NEW YORK

Laws of 1967, chapter 392.

NEVADA

Laws of 1969, chapter 650

NORTH CAROLINA

General Statutes of North Carolina, sections 95-97 through 95-100, article 12.

NORTH DAKOTA

City of Minot vs. Teamsters Local 34, 142 N.W. 2d 612.

OHIO

Ferguson Act, Page's Ohio Revised Code, Laws of 1947, title 41, chapter 4117, sections 4117.01-4117.05.

OKLAHOMA

House Bill 1325, Laws of 1971.
Senate Bill 105, Laws of 1971.

OREGON

Oregon Revised Statutes, sections 243.710-243.760.
Senate Bill 55, Laws of 1969.

PENNSYLVANIA

Senate Bill 1333, Laws of 1970.

SOUTH DAKOTA

Laws of 1970, chapters 3-18.
Senate Bill 121, Laws of 1971.

TENNESSEE

City of Alcoa vs. IBEW, 203 Tenn. 12; 308 S.W. 2d 476.

TEXAS

Attorney General's Opinion, No. M-77, May 18, 1967.
Laws of 1947, article 514E, section 1.

UTAH

Attorney General's Opinion, Oct. 1, 1945.
Attorney General's Opinion, January 12, 1960.

VERMONT

Laws of 1967, Public Act 198.
Laws of 1969, chapter 27.

VIRGINIA

Code of Virginia 1950, title 40, sections 40-65 to 40-67.

WASHINGTON

Laws of 1967, chapter 108.
Laws of 1969, chapter 215.
Laws of 1965, chapter 28.72, Revised Code of Washington, section 28.72.010-.090.
Washington State Personnel Board Merit System Rules, chapter 356.32.

D. S. CHAUHAN, associate professor of public administration at the University of Arkansas, Fayetteville, received his Ph.D. from the University of Lucknow in India. He has served on the faculties of the University of Lucknow and Kent State University. His published articles on public administration have featured his own interest in political-administrative leadership, urban affairs, public management practices, and intergovernmental relations. Coauthor of the Public Health Personnel Policy Handbook *(1974) for the Arkansas State Department of Health, Dr. Chauhan is a departmental editor of the* Midwest Review of Public Administration *and a member of the Committee on Higher Education/Government Relations, American Society of Public Administration.*